The Cub Scout Handbook

The Cub Scout Handbook

Written by

Judy Banks
Sue Burton
Graham Coulson
Norman Garnett
Roger Haywood
Amanda Lea
Greg Stewart
Julie Stewart
Mary Tyrrell
Deann Weeks
Dave Wood

Illustrated by

Martin Aitchison

Edited by

Greg Stewart
Dave Wood

Assistant Editor

Mike Brennan

The help of the following is also acknowledged

Stephen Cousins
David Harrower
Dorothy Kinloch
Mike Lane
Andrew Pearson
Dave Turnbull
Gwyn Turnbull

Designed and typeset by
Tangent Graphic Design Ltd
Bishop's Stortford Herts

© The Scout Association 1990
ISBN 0 85165 235 2

First Edition 1990
First Printing September 1990

Printed by Grosvenor Press
(Portsmouth)

THIS **Cub Scout Handbook**

belongs to

of the _____ Cub Scout Pack.

My address is

My telephone number is

My Six is

My Sixer's name is

My Cub Scout Leader's name is

My Cub Scout Leader's telephone number is

Contents

Welcome to Cub Scouting

THIS COULD BE YOU!

Do you like having fun, making friends, trying new things? You do? Well, you have joined a group of boys and girls who enjoy these things too — they are called Cub Scouts. They meet together regularly to play games, find out about things and to share excitement and adventures.

A small group of Cub Scouts is called a **Six,** and a number of Sixes is called a **Pack.** The Pack usually meets once a week with some grown-ups and is usually led by an **Akela.**

You can find out why the Leader is called this on **page 11.**

The Cub Scouts in your local area form part of a wider Family of Scouts found all over the world. There are Members both younger than you (called **Beaver Scouts**) and older (called **Scouts** and **Venture Scouts**).

What do Cub Scouts do?

Turn the page and find out...

What do Cub Scouts do?

CUB SCOUTS HAVE FUN

play games

gain badges

make a promise

look after themselves

go on outings and visits

go camping and learn about the outdoors

What do Cub Scouts do?

look
after their
surroundings

help others

create things

go hiking

become Scouts

The Cub Scout Membership Award

INTRODUCTION

Welcome to the Cub Scout Pack! To help you get settled into the Pack, here are some activities for you to do that will help you get to know all about Cub Scouting and to make some new friends straight away.

You must complete EACH section of this Award.

To gain your Cub Scout Membership Award you must complete ALL the following sections.

MYSELF
Tell a Leader in the Cub Scout Pack about your hobbies and interests and what you like doing best. ☐

MY SIX
Join a Six and get to know the other members of your Six by taking part in an activity with them. ☐

MY PACK
1. Get to know other Cub Scouts and Leaders by taking part in at least two Pack Meetings. ☐

2. Be told the first Jungle Story and how to take part in the Grand Howl. ☐

MY BADGES
1. Know the meaning of the Badges you will get when you are invested and how to care for your Group scarf. ☐

2. Know how to gain the Cub Scout Awards and Activity Badges. ☐

MY LAW AND PROMISE
1. Know the Cub Scout Law and Promise and talk with a Leader about how you can put them into practice each day. ☐

2. Know the Scout Salute and sign, hand-shake and motto and why we use them. ☐

The Cub Scout Membership Award

As soon as you complete the two activities for your Scout Family Badge you will receive a Scout Family Badge to wear on your uniform.

You will also be given the opportunity to earn three more Scout Family Badges while you are a Cub Scout.

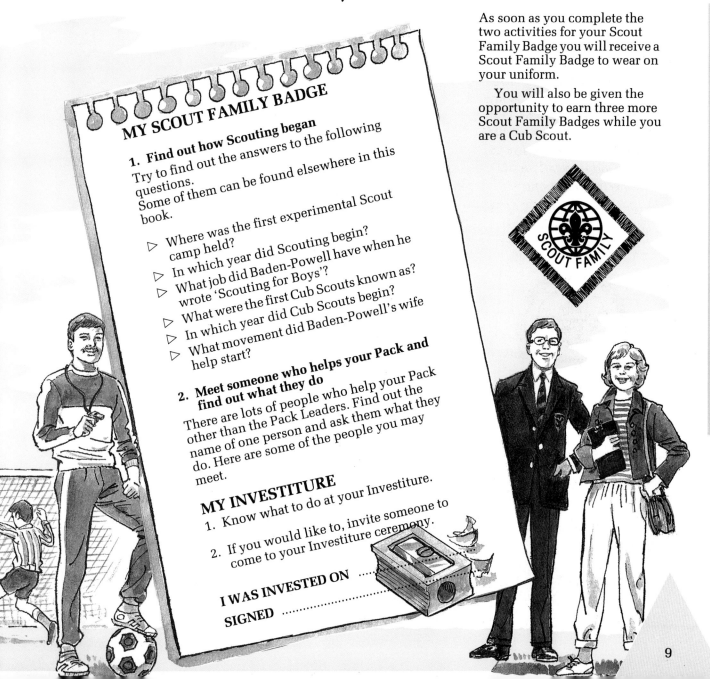

MY SCOUT FAMILY BADGE

1. Find out how Scouting began

Try to find out the answers to the following questions.
Some of them can be found elsewhere in this book.

▷ Where was the first experimental Scout camp held?
▷ In which year did Scouting begin?
▷ What job did Baden-Powell have when he wrote 'Scouting for Boys'?
▷ What were the first Cub Scouts known as?
▷ In which year did Cub Scouts begin?
▷ What movement did Baden-Powell's wife help start?

2. Meet someone who helps your Pack and find out what they do

There are lots of people who help your Pack other than the Pack Leaders. Find out the name of one person and ask them what they do. Here are some of the people you may meet.

MY INVESTITURE

1. Know what to do at your Investiture.

2. If you would like to, invite someone to come to your Investiture ceremony.

I WAS INVESTED ON ....

SIGNED ....

SCOUT FAMILY

The Family of Scouts

When you are invested as a Cub Scout you join a large Family of Scouts. Your Scout Group is part of the Family of Scouts.

Does your Group have all the Sections which make up the Family of Scouts?

Tick the ones which you know are in your Scout Group...

also have their own special badges.

Ask Akela to show you them. Make a rough sketch of them below and colour them in.

TICK	MEETING NIGHT	START TIME	END TIME
☐ Beaver Scout Colony			
☐ Cub Scout Pack			
☐ Scout Troop			
☐ Venture Scout Unit			

Your Group and its Leaders are all looked after by your **Group Scout Leader.**

A special part of the Cub Scout uniform is your Group scarf. This scarf tells everybody to which Group you belong, as each Scout Group has its own coloured scarf.

Did you know that your Group is also part of a much bigger family? It is part of a Scout **District** and Scout **County** or **Area.** Just as you have your Group scarf to show your identity, your Scout District and Scout County or Area may

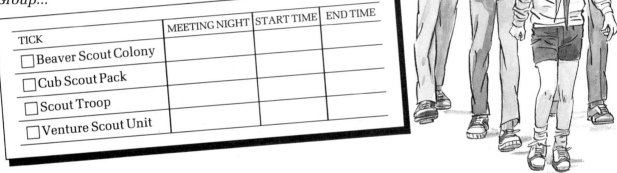

10

The Jungle Book

The Jungle Book was written by Rudyard Kipling and tells the story of how a boy called Mowgli became a member of a wolf cub pack and of the adventures he had in the jungle. In the story, the wolf cubs had a very good and kind leader who was called Akela.

In the Cub Scout Pack, the Leader in charge will usually be called Akela, after the wolf pack

Akela
the leader of the wolf pack

Kaa
the snake

Mowgli
the little boy who joined the pack

Chil
the bird of prey

Hathi
the elephant

Raksha
the mother wolf

Rama
the leader of buffaloes

Bagheera
the black panther

leader, and the other Leaders will often take the names of other characters in the book.

Ask Akela to tell you the first Jungle Story about how Mowgli became a member of the wolf cub pack. When you have heard the story, you should be able to recognise some of the animals and their names shown here.

There is one animal in *The Jungle Book* who is very fierce and scary.

Shade in the enclosed sections of the picture to reveal Shere Khan.

Baloo *the friendly bear*

Shere Khan

How Cub Scouting Began

Many years ago, there was a young boy of about your age who had four brothers. He loved the outdoor life and would often go walking, camping, fishing, tracking and climbing trees.

This boy was called **Robert Baden-Powell** and when he left school, he decided to join the army.

He became an Officer in the army and liked to train his men with competitions and games. He even used one of his tricks to save a town called Mafeking, in South Africa. What he did was

build models of soldiers and stand them up on top of the walls of the town. The people who were attacking the town were scared away because they thought the model soldiers were real.

Since Baden-Powell had only a few soldiers in Mafeking, he often used local boys to help with first aid, carrying messages and running errands.

When he came back to England, he found out that he was being called a hero because of his bravery in South Africa. Soon after he returned to England, Baden-Powell wrote a book about training in the army called *Aids to Scouting*. He found out that boys liked to read these stories and try out the skills for themselves.

As an experiment, in 1907 Baden-Powell ran a camp for 20 boys from different backgrounds, at a place called Brownsea Island in Dorset. The

boys enjoyed the games, sports and other activities at the camp so much that Baden-Powell decided to write down all his ideas in another book, called ***Scouting for Boys.*** This book was written in six parts like a magazine and very soon, boys all over the United Kingdom had formed themselves into groups of 'Boy Scouts' and had asked adults to run Scouting activities for them.

how to light fires and cook meals.

Scouting grew and grew and in 1920 Baden-Powell became World Chief Scout. Nine years later, he became Lord Baden-Powell of Gilwell.

After his death in 1941, Scouting continued to change with the times. In 1967 Wolf Cubs became 'Cub Scouts' and a Venture Scout Section was

introduced to replace Rover Scouts and Senior Scouts.

In 1986, Beaver Scouts were welcomed as full Members of The Scout Association and in 1990 girls were allowed to become Cub Scouts — who knows what other changes will take place as you go through the Scout Movement?

Every year, Scouts and Guides across the world celebrate the birthday of Lord Baden-Powell. Can you find out what date this is?

It was not long before the younger brothers of these early Scouts began to ask to join in the fun of Scouting. In 1916, Baden-Powell started a special Section called the Wolf Cubs for boys aged between eight and eleven. They learned all sorts of exciting and useful things like first aid, tracking, how to keep themselves fit and healthy and

WORLD SCOUTING TODAY

Like all good ideas, lots of boys and girls have tried Scouting and today there are Scouts in nearly every part of the world.

During your time with your Cub Scout Pack you will find out more about these Scouts in other countries. Not all Cub Scouts wear a uniform like yours, and some even make a different Promise.

Whatever Scouts are doing and wherever they are, you will always be able to recognise them. How? Well, when they are in uniform they will all be wearing the same badge — The World Badge.

The Cub Scout Promise and Law

All Members of the Scout Movement make a special Promise. When you are invested as a Cub Scout you will have to know the Cub Scout Law and you will also have to make your Promise in front of the Pack.

It is easy to learn and say these words, but it is really important that you try to keep your Promise every day. Helping other people means helping them at all times — not just when you feel like it.

Doing your best means trying your hardest all the time — and in everything you do. Doing your duty to God and the Queen really means that you respect

THE CUB SCOUT PROMISE

I promise that I will do my best,
to do my duty to God and to the Queen,
to help other people
and to keep the Cub Scout Law.

your God, the world in which we live, other people and the laws of the land in which you

THE CUB SCOUT LAW

A Cub Scout always does his best,
thinks of others before himself and
does a good turn every day.

live. It means behaving properly to all those you meet every day.

A good Cub Scout is not selfish but tries to find ways of helping other people. A Good Turn is something you do to help someone else. Every Cub Scout is challenged to do at least one Good Turn every day.

You will see that doing your best is mentioned in both the Promise and the Law. That is because it is very important. If you want to be a good Cub Scout there is no other way — you simply **have** to do your best.

Ceremonies

The Salute

All Members of the Scout Movement use the same salute, although Beaver Scouts do not have any salute at all. The salute is made with the right hand and only when you are standing at the Alert. It is both a greeting and a sign of respect.

The three fingers of the salute remind you of your Promise to do your duty to God and the Queen and to help other people. Your Leader will tell you when you use the salute in your Pack.

The Scout Sign

The Scout Sign is almost the same as the salute, but you should hold your hand at shoulder height. It is only used when someone is making or renewing their Promise.

The Scout Motto

Being a Cub Scout, you will always want to be prepared for anything.

You should be prepared to.....
- ▷ help other people
- ▷ keep yourself fit and healthy
- ▷ make new friends
- ▷ keep the Cub Scout Promise and Law

The Handshake

When Scouts meet, they greet each other in a special way. They shake hands with the left hand! You will often see Akela using the left handshake – especially when a badge is presented. There is a very good reason for using the left handshake.

When Baden-Powell was a soldier in Africa, he saw lots of tribal chiefs who carried spears and shields. He noticed that it was a sign of great trust to offer your left hand when shaking hands. This was because you had to put down your shield and yet leave the other person with a spear in his hand.

The Grand Howl

You may have seen Cub Scouts doing the Grand Howl. It is a very special way of saying 'hello' to Akela and a way of reminding you about your Cub Scout Promise every time you do it.

When you have made your Promise and been invested as a Cub Scout, you will be able to join in the Grand Howl.

Cub Scouts start by forming a circle, with Akela standing in the middle. The Grand Howl begins when Akela's arms are raised and then lowered. The Pack squats down like the wolves did and call out:

Akela, we'll do our best!'

The Cubs then jump up, stand at the alert and the Duty Sixer salutes Akela and calls out:

'Cubs! Do your best!'

With a smart salute, the Cubs all call back:

'We WILL do our best!'

Ceremonies

Flag Ceremonies

Usually, straight after the Grand Howl has taken place, the Pack faces the Union Flag.

The Duty Sixer will walk to the flag and pull a string to let the flag fly freely — this is called 'breaking the flag'. Everybody salutes the flag at the same time as the Duty Sixer to show their loyalty to the Queen and to the country in which they are living.

At the end of the Meeting, the Cub Scouts face the flag after the Grand Howl and stand at the alert while the flag is lowered by the Duty Sixer.

How to Stand

Cub Scouts try to look as smart as they can whenever they are in uniform. To help them to look even smarter, they have two special ways of standing — one is called 'Alert' and the other is called 'At Ease'.

A Leader or a Sixer will call out the commands — try to see how smartly you can do the actions.

When a Leader or Sixer calls **'Pack Alert'** or **'Six Alert'**, you should stand up straight with your arms smartly by your sides moving your **left** leg to put your feet together.

When a Leader calls **'Pack — at Ease'** you should move your **left** leg until it is comfortably apart from the other, with your hands held behind your back. Practice standing at Alert and At Ease.

Your Uniform

Your uniform tells everyone that you are a Cub Scout and to which Pack you belong. The Uniform is a green long-sleeved sweatshirt or T-shirt, long or short grey trousers and for girls, grey skirts plus the items you are given at your Investiture. If you wear shorts for Cubs, you also wear long grey socks with green garter tabs to keep them up.

Your Investiture

Your Investiture is a very important occasion for the whole Pack. It is a special time for you to say that you are ready to make your Promise and become a full Member and for the other Cub Scouts to welcome you properly.

You may want to invite your parents or guardians and Akela may invite the Group Scout Leader to the ceremony as it is an important event and one in which they may want to be involved.

Before your investiture, Akela will make sure that you know what you are going to say and do for your special moment.

It will go something like this, although your Pack may have its own way of doing some things.....

Your Sixer will bring you to Akela and say that you are ready to become a Cub Scout.

Akela *'Do you want to be a Cub Scout?'*

You *'Yes Akela, I do'.*

Akela *'What is the Cub Scout Law?'*

You *'A Cub Scout always does his best, thinks of others before himself and does a good turn every day.'*

Akela *'Are you ready to make your Cub Scout Promise?'*

You *'Yes Akela, I am.'*

Akela *'Pack, make the Scout Sign.'*

You will make the Scout Sign along with all the others and say the Promise. Akela may say the Promise a bit at a time and you will repeat it. Then Akela will shake you by the left hand to welcome you into the Pack.

Akela *'I trust you to do your best to keep this Promise. You are now a Cub Scout in the worldwide brotherhood of Scouts.'*

Now you will be given your badges and Group scarf. You salute Akela and turn to salute the Pack before you return to your place in the Grand Howl circle.

17

Badges and Awards

As a Cub Scout there will be plenty to do and talk about, in small groups and with the whole Pack. The activities in which you take part are usually part of the Cub Scout Training Scheme, and as you move through the Scheme you will be able to gain badges to wear on your uniform.

The details of all of the badges can be found in this book along with some suggestions as to how you can gain them.

So how do you start?

Membership Award

The first Award you will be working towards will be your Cub Scout Membership Award. Details of this can be found on pages 8 and 9.

This will help you to find out what being a Cub Scout is all about. When you have gained this you can move on to:

The Cub Scout Award

This will give you an idea of the type of activities which you can try during your time in the Cub Scout Pack. The details of this start on page 20.

When you have gained these awards you can begin to look at:

Adventure Awards

These are each broken up into ten parts. Some will tell you what you have to do and others give you a choice of activities. You will get help from your Leaders with choosing something to do which you will find interesting and fun.

The ten areas are:

▷ Outdoor Scouting
▷ Sports and Hobbies
▷ Helping Others
▷ Looking after Yourself
▷ Science and Nature
▷ Creativity
▷ Your Community
▷ Countries and Cultures
▷ Your Promise
▷ The Family of Scouts

There are four Scout Family Badges that you can earn at different stages. These will help you to understand how big our Scout Family is and to meet some of the other members of that Family.

You will find what you need to do for these badges at the end of each of the sections about the four Awards — see pages 9, 26, 51 and 85.

CUB SCOUT AWARD

MEMBERSHIP AWARD

ACTIVITY BADGES

Badges and Awards

The Cub Scout Challenge

When you get to be 9½ years old you will probably want to start doing different sorts of things from the younger Cub Scouts. Just for you there is a special **Cub Scout Challenge** waiting.

This is full of activities just like all the other Awards and badges but these ones have been specially thought up to show that you are one of the older Cub Scouts and are able to do more on your own and to help plan and run activities for others too.

You must complete the requirements of ALL of the FOUR Sections.

> ▷ Outdoor Challenge
> ▷ Adventure Challenge
> ▷ Sharing Together
> ▷ Helping to Lead

Full details of this Challenge can be found on page 86.

Activity Badges

As a Cub Scout you may already have your own hobbies and interests, or you may like to try something new. To help you do this there are some special **Activity Badges** which you can earn on your own and some by working with a group of friends. These are all listed towards the end of this book, starting on page 98.

Where are you going to start?

Just turn the page and enter the world of the Cub Scout...

MEMBERSHIP AWARD

ADVENTURE AWARD

ADVENTURE CREST AWARD

CUB SCOUT CHALLENGE

ACTIVITY BADGES

The Cub Scout Award

INTRODUCTION

This is the very first of the Awards and you can start working for it as soon as you join.

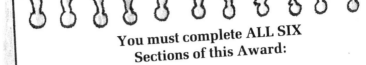

You must complete ALL SIX
Sections of this Award:

DATE COMPLETED

▷ Tracking

▷ Country Code

▷ Good Turns

▷ First Aid

▷ My Promise

▷ Scout Family Badge

Remember...
The Scout Family Badge

SCOUT FAMILY

Tracking

1. Follow a trail (out of doors if possible).

Tracking signs are used to leave a trail for people to follow. Only those who know tracking signs will be able to read the clues and follow the trail. It is like a secret code and the signs are usually made out of sticks, stones and other natural materials.

2. Either
a) Lay a trail for others to follow
Or
b) Make a chart or model showing tracking signs.

A trail does not always have to be in the countryside — you could lay a trail around your Headquarters using sticks and stones. If you live in a town perhaps you could use chalk signs on the pavement (as long as you clean them off afterwards). Sometimes a trail can be made using things such as sand, wood, matches, sticky paper stuck on walls, or pieces of wool in bushes. Try to make up a trail of your own but remember not to leave any litter.

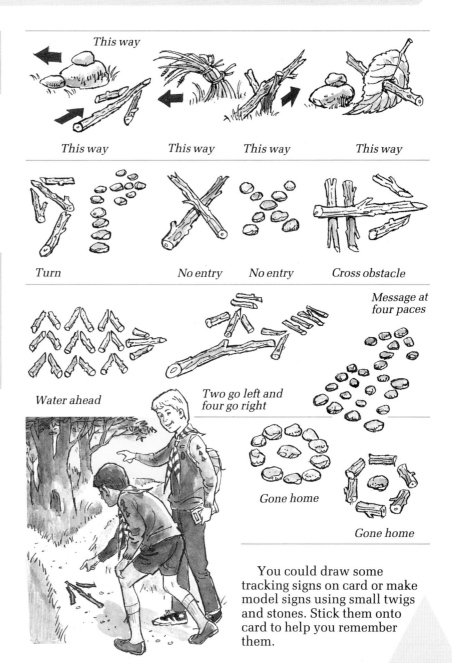

This way

This way   *This way*   *This way*   *This way*

Turn   *No entry*   *No entry*   *Cross obstacle*

Message at four paces

Water ahead   *Two go left and four go right*

Gone home

Gone home

You could draw some tracking signs on card or make model signs using small twigs and stones. Stick them onto card to help you remember them.

21

Country Code

1. Find out about the Country Code.

Here is the Country Code.

1. Enjoy the countryside and respect its life and work.
2. Guard against all risks of fire.
3. Fasten all gates.
4. Keep your dogs under close control.
5. Keep to public paths across farmland.
6. Use gates and stiles to cross fences, hedges and walls.
7. Leave livestock, crops and machinery alone.
8. Take your litter home.
9. Help to keep all water clean.
10. Protect wildlife, plants and trees.
11. Take special care on country roads.
12. Make no unnecessary noise.

Read this through with a Leader or other Cub Scouts and say why you think it is important to have each part of the Country Code. Which one item do you think is the most important? Tell the other Cubs your reasons. Do your friends agree with your choice?

2. Either
a) As part of a Pack activity out of doors, show you know the Country Code
Or
b) Make a poster to tell others about part of the Country Code.

Cubs Scouts are always interested in getting outside for fun and adventure. This is even better if you can go into the countryside. If we all keep the Country Code our countryside will stay beautiful for us to enjoy. If you see the Country Code being broken, try to make it better by picking up litter and so on.

You could make a poster about part of the Country Code.

Can the other Cub Scouts guess which part of the Code you have drawn?

Good Turns

1. Keep a diary of good turns for a week showing how you have helped other people.

As a Cub Scout you have made a Promise to help other people, and do a Good Turn every day. There are lots of ways in which you can do this. A Good Turn is a special job you do for someone that you might not normally do.

Sometimes you can help others in a secret way, without them realising that you are trying hard to be helpful.

MY **GOOD TURN** DIARY

DAY 1

DAY 2

DAY 3

DAY 4

DAY 5

DAY 6

DAY 7

You could try playing quietly when your mum has a headache or picking up litter that someone else dropped.

Note your secret good turn in your diary.

First Aid

1. Know the importance of first aid and know how and when to get adult help.

It is important that someone does something to help an injured person, so that the injury does not get any worse.

If you find someone who is injured and needs help, the most important thing you as a Cub Scout can do is to tell a grown-up as soon as possible. You may be able to shout or go for help, but occasionally you will need to use the telephone.

Can you use a telephone? Akela will help you make a telephone call to a parent or other adult to practise what you should do in real life. Never dial 999 unless it is a real emergency though.

In any first aid situation, once you have called for help, you can make the patient feel better by saying that help is on the way and that they are going to be alright.

2. Take part in a first aid activity or game.

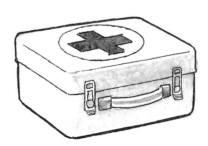

Your leader may ask you to tackle a simple first aid incident. This might involve cuts and grazes, nose bleeds and burns or scalds.

Remember not to play around during a pretend incident – you will need to practise being calm and sensible for when you might have to do real first aid.

My Promise

1. Make up and share a simple prayer using words or pictures about your hobbies, your family, your friends or anything you would like to talk to God about.

God is your friend and He wants you to talk to Him. A prayer is your way of talking with God. Sometimes you will say prayers altogether in the Pack, perhaps at the end of a Pack Meeting, when you thank God for the fun you have had. Sometimes you will say prayers quietly so that no one else hears. You might say 'Please God', 'Thank you God' or 'Sorry God,' when you think you could be in trouble.

God likes you to tell Him about the things you like, the things that make you sad and the things you are sorry for.

In the space above draw a picture or cut out a picture from a newspaper or magazine, and write a short prayer about it to God.

My prayer ....
....
....
....
....

2. When you have finished most of the activities for the Cub Scout Award, talk to a Leader about how you have tried to put your Promise and Law into practice in everything you have done.

When you were invested you promised to do your best. Think about all the things you have done since you made the Promise, and try to make a list of the times where you really did your best.

This list might help you think of ways in which you have helped other people. Add your own ideas to the list.

▷ Helping at home.

▷ Helping your Six.

▷ Doing your good turns.

▷ Playing fair in games.

▷ Taking care not to drop litter.

▷ ....

▷ ....

▷ ....

▷ ....

Talk about your list with a Leader.

25

Scout Family Badge

As soon as you complete these two activities, you will receive a Scout Family Badge to wear on your uniform.

1. Find out something about each of the Sections in The Scout Association, either in your own Group or elsewhere in the District.

What do you know about the other Sections?

▷ Does everyone wear the same uniform?

▷ What age do you have to be before joining each Section?

▷ Do all Sections make the same Promise?

▷ What type of activities do the other Sections take part in?

2. Take part in either a Group, District or County/Area activity or take part in a joint Pack meeting with another Cub Scout Pack.

There will be lots of opportunities for you to meet new Cub Scouts outside of your own Cub Scout Pack and take part in activities with them.

Cub Scouts from your District will meet together sometimes for activity days and other events.

Perhaps you will have a chance to join the Cub Scouts in your County or Area for a big activity day or camp.

SPONSORED WALK

START

CUB SCOUT AWARD
THIS IS TO CERTIFY

NAME ....

OF THE ....
has completed the Cub Scout Award. satisfactorily.

SIGNED .... AKELA

DATE ....

The Adventure Award

Now that you have completed your Cub Scout Award and seen some of the exciting things that Cub Scouts do, you are ready to start your Adventure Award.

You must complete each section of this Award.

50m

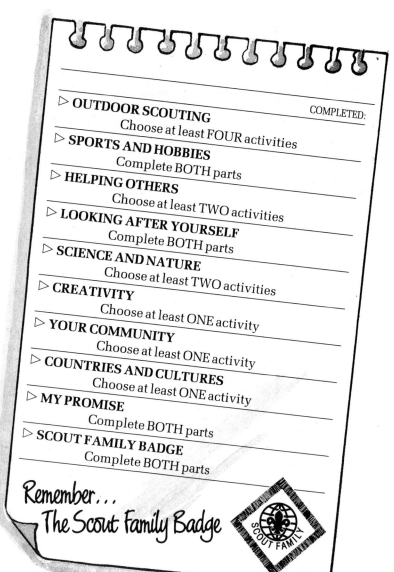

COMPLETED:

▷ **OUTDOOR SCOUTING**
Choose at least FOUR activities

▷ **SPORTS AND HOBBIES**
Complete BOTH parts

▷ **HELPING OTHERS**
Choose at least TWO activities

▷ **LOOKING AFTER YOURSELF**
Complete BOTH parts

▷ **SCIENCE AND NATURE**
Choose at least TWO activities

▷ **CREATIVITY**
Choose at least ONE activity

▷ **YOUR COMMUNITY**
Choose at least ONE activity

▷ **COUNTRIES AND CULTURES**
Choose at least ONE activity

▷ **MY PROMISE**
Complete BOTH parts

▷ **SCOUT FAMILY BADGE**
Complete BOTH parts

Remember...
The Scout Family Badge

SCOUT FAMILY

The Adventure Award

Checklist

OUTDOOR SCOUTING

You must choose at least FOUR activities from this section.

1. MAPPING ☐
2. OUTDOOR COOKING ☐
3. KNOTS ☐
4. COMPASS ☐
5. HIKING ☐
6. MINI-PIONEERING ☐
7. CAMPING ☐

SPORTS AND HOBBIES

You must complete BOTH parts in this section.

1. SPORTSMANLIKE ATTITUDE ☐
2. CHOOSE TWO SPORTS OR HOBBIES ☐

HELPING OTHERS

You must choose at least TWO activities from this section.

1. FIRST AID ☐
2. WATER SAFETY ☐
3. HOME SAFETY ☐
4. SPECIAL GOOD TURNS ☐
5. HELPING AKELA ☐

LOOKING AFTER YOURSELF

You must complete BOTH parts in this section.

1. YOUR BELONGINGS ☐
2. ROAD SAFETY ☐

SCIENCE AND NATURE

You must choose at least TWO activities from this section

1. SCIENCE EXPERIMENTS ☐
2. STARS AND PLANETS ☐
3. GROWING THINGS ☐
4. WEATHER ☐
5. THE NATURAL WORLD ☐

CREATIVITY

You must choose at least ONE activity from this section.

1. ACTING ☐
2. MUSIC ☐
3. WORSHIP ☐
4. PUPPETS ☐
5. REPORTERS ☐
6. PAINTING AND DRAWING ☐
7. MAGIC ☐
8. TAKING PICTURES ☐
9. CRAFTS ☐
10 OVER TO YOU... ☐
    (a chance to choose your own activity not in this list).

YOUR COMMUNITY

You must choose at least ONE activity from this section.

1. LOCAL FEATURES ☐
2. LOCAL SURVEY ☐
3. LOCAL HISTORY ☐
4. LOCAL TRANSPORT ☐
5. LOCAL VISIT ☐
6. LOCAL PEOPLE ☐

COUNTRIES AND CULTURES

You must choose at least ONE activity from this section.

1. CUSTOMS AND TRADITIONS ☐
2. ROYAL FAMILY ☐
3. FLAGS AND SAINTS ☐
4. NATIONAL CHARITY ☐

MY PROMISE

You must complete BOTH parts in this section.

1. PRAYER POSTER ☐
2. TALK WITH LEADER ☐

SCOUT FAMILY BADGE

You must complete BOTH parts in this section.

1. FIND OUT ABOUT SCOUT ACTIVITIES ☐
2. AN EVENT WITH OTHER SECTIONS ☐

Outdoor Scouting

INTRODUCTION

This is a chance for you to learn some outdoor Scouting skills, or perhaps to improve some you already know.

You must choose at least FOUR out of the seven activities in this section.

1. MAPPING
Know at least eight map symbols and be able to find them on an Ordnance Survey map.

The Ordnance Survey maps use a very simple set of pictures and letters (called symbols) to show where things like churches, telephone boxes and car parks can be found.

Try to draw a line to match each map symbol with a picture of what you would actually see on a walk....

2. OUTDOOR COOKING
Cook something on an open fire.

An adult will help you to build and light a fire at camp or during a visit to the country — or even on a Pack night.

Remember not to start cooking until the flames have died down and you are left with red glowing embers. Remember to be careful, as fire will not just burn the wood but can burn you as well.

Here are some things you could cook on your fire...

▷ Pancakes
▷ Spud-eggs
▷ Dough twists
▷ Sausage kebab
▷ Baked potatoes
▷ Toasted marshmallows

Badge link

WHY NOT TRY THE CAMPER BADGE?

3. KNOTS
Learn how to tie at least two knots and use them to take part in a game.

Here are some knots you might like to learn:

THE REEF KNOT

This is a strong, flat knot, used to tie bandages and slings in first aid. It is also used to join two ends of string or rope together, such as on a parcel.

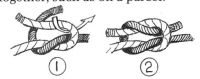

Practise this knot by sticking different coloured tape over each end of a piece of string.

Green over white and under. White over green and under.

SHEET BEND

This is a good knot for tying a piece of string to a piece of rope, without the knot slipping undone. It is also used for tying a line to a flag.

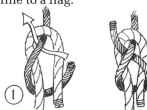

And don't forget to hank the rope neatly when you have finished tying your knots.

Outdoor Scouting

4. COMPASS
Know the eight points of the compass and use them to take part in a game.

The main points are

> North
> South
> East
> West

The points in between are

> North West
> North East
> South West
> South East

Can you mark these points on the compass? The first two are done for you.

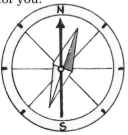

WHY NOT TRY THE NAVIGATOR BADGE?

5. HIKING
Go on a short hike and know what to wear and take with you.

When you go for a hike with your friends, remember to always have an adult with you.

What else should you take with you on a short day hike? Use a black pen to fill in the box of any item you would leave at home.

Waterproof coat

Money for telephone

Soft drink (not fizzy)

Watch

Tent

Pocket first aid kit

Sleeping bag

Sandals

Torch

Radio

Compass

Map

Binoculars

Strong shoes

Packed lunch

A deckchair

similar bag which you have to carry in your hands or else your arms will get very tired.

If you have crossed out the right things, you should see the face of a happy hiker!

Be sure to carry these in a small rucsac or daysac — do not use a plastic carrier bag or

WHY NOT TRY THE EXPLORER BADGE?

*Choose at least **four** activities in Outdoor Scouting*

Outdoor Scouting

6. MINI PIONEERING
Build something using garden canes, elastic bands and string.

Pioneering is the name for building things with sticks. In the Scout Troop you may use large poles and thick rope to build real bridges, swings and so on.

You could build one of the following models using thin sticks held together with elastic bands and string — or maybe you could invent something of your own...

▷ A bridge
▷ A star
▷ A gate
▷ A flag pylon

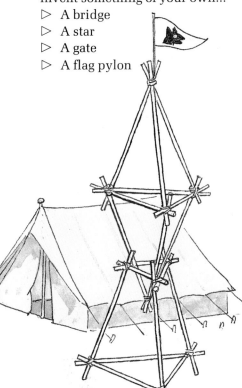

7. CAMPING
Help pitch a tent and know how to take care of it.

There are all sorts of different types of tents, so make sure you know how to pitch it properly before you start.

Here is a Patrol Tent — you will probably use one of these at a Cub or Scout camp.

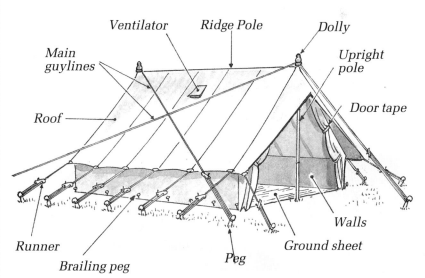

Ventilator   Ridge Pole   Dolly
Main guylines   Upright pole
Roof   Door tape
Runner   Brailing peg   Peg   Ground sheet   Walls

When camping, remember these important points to stop any damage happening to the tent and to help you have a comfortable night's sleep...

▷ Lay the groundsheets over the top of the brown cloth which runs along the bottom of the tent.

▷ Do not touch the inside of the tent when it is raining or it will leak.
▷ Do not run around the inside or outside of the tent or you may trip over and damage it.
▷ Fasten the tent properly when you leave it.
▷ Keep your bag and clothes on the groundsheet and away from the sides of the tent at all times.
▷ Do not keep or eat food in the tent or you will attract insects and small animals.

Badge link

WHY NOT TRY THE CAMPER BADGE?

THE ADVENTURE AWARD

*Choose at least **four** activities in Outdoor Scouting*

INTRODUCTION

In this section you will have the chance to share with other Cub Scouts your favourite Sport or Hobby, and also to try a new one.

You must complete BOTH parts of this section.

1. Show a sportsmanlike attitude in all Pack games and activities and know why this is important.

2. Choose at least two sports or hobbies. Choose one which you already do — tell other Cub Scouts and Leaders what you have done recently to improve or develop your hobby or sport. Try one which is new to you.

It feels good to take part in a race and do well in it doesn't it?

How do you feel when you do not win even though you have done your best?

How do your friends feel? How do you feel when someone in your Six does his best, but you still do not win?

What can you do to help everyone feel better about it?

What can you say to help everyone feel glad that they took part?

There are all sorts of sports and hobbies you could choose for this Section. Here's a list to start you thinking...

A athletics/archery/American football/art/aircraft

B book reading/basketball/baseball/bird watching/bell ringing

C chess/cycling/computers/cooking/choir/canoeing/collections

D drama/dancing/drawing/diving

E exploring/entertaining/electronics

F football/fencing/fishing

G gardening/golf

H horse riding/hiking/hockey/high jumping

I indoor sports/ice skating/illusions

J judo/jogging

K kite making/karate/knotting/keep fit

L long-jumping

M mechanics/music/matchbox collecting/macramé/magic/marbles

N netball/needlecraft

O origami/orienteering

P pets/poetry/painting/pool

Q quizzes

R reading/rugby/rambling/running

S stamps/star gazing/swimming/skiing/snooker/singing

T T-shirt printing/tennis/trampolining/train spotting

U underwater plants

V visiting museums/volleyball

W walking/writing

X xylophone playing

Y yoga/Youth Hostelling

Z zoo clubs

▷ What can I do now? ....

....

▷ What am I going to try and improve? ....

....

Discuss with a Leader what you are going to do.

*Do **both** activities in Sports and Hobbies.*

Helping Others

INTRODUCTION

As a Cub Scout you have made a Promise to help other people at all times. This section will give you the chance to do activities which will help others.

You must choose at least TWO of the five activities in this section.

1. FIRST AID

Show you know how to apply simple first aid and know how to make a patient comfortable and reassure them.

You will remember from your Cub Scout Award that it is important to fetch adult help as quickly as possible if someone is hurt, but sometimes you will need to help people yourself if the injury is not very serious.

NOSE BLEEDS

To treat a nose bleed, pinch the soft part of the nose, just below the bone and keep the head tipped forward. You must keep pinching the nose until it stops bleeding. Tell the person to breathe through their mouth until the bleeding stops and not to blow their nose for several hours so the blood clot is not disturbed.

CUTS AND GRAZES

If the skin is cut, germs can get in, so cleaning the wound is very important. You must use clean water and cotton wool or antiseptic wipes and wipe away from the centre of the wound. When you have done that you should cover the cut with a plaster.

BURNS AND SCALDS

A burn is caused by dry heat such as a flame or hot iron. A scald is caused by wet heat such as boiling water or steam. The treatment for a burn or scald is to place the injured part under a cold running tap for about ten minutes or until the pain has stopped.

▷ Do not use ointment or creams
▷ Do not burst blisters
▷ Do not remove burnt clothing

REMEMBER. If the burn, scald, cut or nose bleed is a bad one, you must get adult help as the patient may need to go to hospital.

In any first aid situation you must remember to make the patient comfortable and to talk to them. This will help them feel better.

WHY NOT TRY THE FIRST AID BADGE?

*Choose at least **two** activities in Helping Others.*

Helping Others

2. WATER SAFETY

Know the basic water safety rules and tell others about water safety by drawing a poster, making up an activity or sketch or making up a game.

Water can be great fun but any water can be very dangerous if you do not take great care. If you cannot swim yet, you should try to learn to swim before you leave Cubs. You must also learn and follow the water code.

IF YOU ARE IN A SWIMMING POOL....

▷ Do not push people into the water or swim in the diving area.

- Wait at least an hour after eating food before swimming
- Always follow the advice of the lifeguards
- Do not show off!
- If you feel tired or cold get out of the water
- Never dive into unknown waters
- At the seaside, find out where it is safe to swim
- Do not use inflatable airbeds in the sea

▷ Do not run round the pool as you could slip and hurt yourself.
▷ Never push people's heads under the water.

Tell other Cub Scouts about water safety by:
▷ Making a poster
▷ Performing a mime on water safety
▷ Making up a game for other Cub Scouts to play, based on water safety.

WHY NOT TRY THE SWIMMER BADGE?

3. HOME SAFETY

Know the common causes of accidents in the home and how to prevent them and tell others about home safety by drawing a poster, making up an activity or sketch or making up a game.

Is your home a safe place in which to live?

Draw a simple plan of your bedroom and show it to a Leader or another Cub

Scout. Look for any dangers that may be in your bedroom such as:

▷ toys on the floor
▷ clutter on the window ledges
▷ lots of boxes on top of cupboards which could fall on you
▷ frayed wires
▷ too many plugs in the sockets

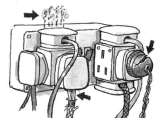

▷ sharp scissors or model knives lying around

With an adult go around your home and note down any danger points. Mark on a diagram the electricity and gas meters and all the electric sockets in your home.

WHY NOT TRY THE HOME SAFETY BADGE?

*Choose at least **two** activities in Helping Others.*

Helping Others

4. SPECIAL GOOD TURNS
Carry out a special good turn for someone who needs help which involves you in extra time or effort.

You could try one of these:
▷ Visit an elderly neighbour and do some jobs to help
▷ Help paint a garden fence
▷ Clean out some cupboards
▷ Help your brother or sister keep their room tidy
▷ Look after someone's pet or plants while they are on holiday

▷ Plant a 'smell' garden for a blind person

Badge link

WHY NOT TRY THE HOME HELP BADGE?

5. HELPING AKELA
Do something special to help a Leader during a Pack Meeting or activity.

Ask Akela what you can do to help.

For example:
▷ Look after and welcome a new Cub Scout.
▷ Lead the prayers at a Pack Meeting
▷ Arrive early to help get ready for a Pack Meeting
▷ Sweep up and help leave the Headquarters tidy
▷ Carry the first aid box on a hike or outing
▷ Fold the flag ready for flag break

*Choose at least **two** activities in Helping Others.*

Looking after Yourself

INTRODUCTION

These activities will give you the chance to show that you are able to look after yourself.

You must complete BOTH activities in this section.

1. YOUR BELONGINGS

Show you can keep your room tidy, look after your clothes and help pack your kit for a camp, holiday or outing.

A good Cub Scout keeps his room tidy and makes his bed each morning. You can learn to fold your clothes or hang them up. Make sure you know the best way to pack your things when going on a holiday or an outing.

Find a safe place to cross away from parked cars.

Stop and wait near the kerb.

Look all around and listen.

And let traffic pass...

If no traffic is near, walk straight across.

Keep looking and listening.

2. ROAD SAFETY

Show you know how to behave as a pedestrian and how and where to cross the road safely.

Roads are dangerous places. Every Cub Scout should know how to cross them safely. Use a crossing if there is one nearby.

You must stop on the pavement, and drivers need to see you clearly. Remember to always wear light colours at night so that you are seen more easily in the dark.

WHY NOT TRY THE PERSONAL SAFETY BADGE?

*Do **both** activities in Looking After Yourself.*

Science and Nature

INTRODUCTION

This section will help you to find out more about the world around you, by using science and by looking more closely at nature.

You must choose at least TWO of the five activities in this section.

1. SCIENCE EXPERIMENTS
Carry out three simple experiments and explain what happens.

You will need to follow the experiments exactly and watch very carefully so you can record what happens.

There will be lots of ideas for experiments in books from your school or local library.

Here are two examples – but try to find out about, and do, three more experiments of your own.

SINKING AND FLOATING

You will need: Some modelling clay, a bowl and water.

What you do: Roll the modelling clay up into a ball and place it in a bowl of water.

What happens?

Now roll the clay into a flat sheet and model it into a boat shape, pinching the corners so that no water can get in. Place this into the water.

What happens?

Conclusion: When the clay is rolled up there is no air inside it and, because it is heavier than water, it sinks. However, when it is modelled into a boat shape, its surface area displaces the water which keeps it afloat.

STRING TELEPHONE

You will need: Two empty yoghurt pots and a piece of string at least 10 metres long.

What you do: Pierce carefully a small hole in the bottom of each pot and push one end of the string through each, tying a knot on the inside of the pot as shown below.

Ask a friend to hold one pot while you hold the other. Keeping the string tight, speak into your pot and your friend will hear you through his pot.

Conclusion: When we speak, the molecules in the air hit against each other and transmit the sound over a distance. With the string telephone, the string vibrates and carries the sound along it from one end to the other.

Badge link

WHY NOT TRY THE SCIENTIST BADGE?

*Choose at least **two** activities in Science and Nature.*

Science and Nature

2. STARS AND PLANETS

Find out some information about the stars and/or the planets, if possible using a telescope or a pair of binoculars, and show it to other Cub Scouts.

You may know an adult who will let you use a telescope or binoculars to look at the stars more closely. If not, it is still possible to see stars on a dark clear night, especially in the winter. **Remember, however, *never* to look directly at the sun as this would damage your eyes.**

There are lots of books which show you diagrams of special patterns of stars — CONSTELLATIONS — which you can then find in the sky. They have special names such as THE PLOUGH and THE LITTLE BEAR. Many constellations have stories about how they got their names. Try to find out about Orion and the other constellations.

You may be able to visit a Planetarium or Science museum to find out more.

Try to find out the names of the other planets in the Solar System. Which one is nearest to the sun? Which planet is the biggest? What is the furthest place from Earth visited by man?

Badge link

WHY NOT TRY THE ASTRONOMER BADGE?

3. GROWING THINGS

Grow a plant and know what conditions are needed for plants to grow.

This is a chance for you to grow a plant in a garden, window box or pot. You may like to grow a flower or something to eat. You could have a competition with another Cub Scout to see who can grow the tallest sunflower.

Young plants need the right conditions to grow properly.

You could try a simple experiment to find out about the best growing conditions. Put some cress seeds in two dishes lined with damp kitchen paper or blotting paper and put both in a dark cupboard for one or two days. Then take one out and put it by a window. You will need to keep the paper damp all the time. After a few days, you will see how important sunlight is for healthy plant growth.

Badge link

WHY NOT TRY THE GARDENER BADGE?

*Choose at least **two** activities in Science and Nature.*

Science and Nature

4. WEATHER
Keep a weather log for at least two weeks and display your findings.

The four main things which affect the weather are the sun, the atmosphere, water vapour and the wind. These all work together, spreading the sun's heat around the world and making clouds, rain and snow. It happens all the time around us.

You should make a simple record of the weather − A WEATHER LOG − every day for at least two weeks.

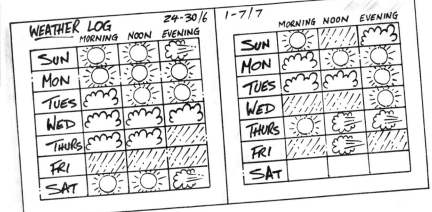

You could make a weather log using the special pictures you see on the television weather forecasts.

It will be interesting to keep your weather log and compare the forecast with the real weather. Did they forecast the weather you recorded?

5. THE NATURAL WORLD
Display something you have found out about the life-cycle and habitat of any bird, animal, fish, insect, tree or plant.

Find out about the life of a bird, animal, fish, insect, tree or plant that you see around you.
See if you can find out:
▷ what it eats
▷ where it lives (its habitat)
▷ how it feeds
▷ what are its enemies

See if you can find out:
▷ where it grows
▷ what shape its leaves are

▷ if it has a scent
▷ how it reproduces
▷ how the seeds are spread
▷ what damages the plant

Draw some pictures, collect photographs and write about the life cycle of your chosen plant or animal so that you can share this with other Cub Scouts.

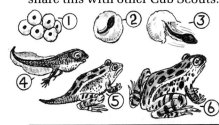

Badge link

WHY NOT TRY THE NATURALIST BADGE?

*Choose at least **two** activities in Science and Nature.*

Creativity

INTRODUCTION

Here you can use your imagination in either funny or serious activities. It is a chance to dress up, to entertain friends, or to show them a special skill you have learned.

You must choose at least ONE of the ten activities in this section.

1. ACTING
Contribute to and take part in a sketch or mime.

Acting is great fun. Take part in a short sketch with other members of your Six or Pack. The sketch can be either a short play or a mime.

A mime is acting without any words, using your hands, arms and your face to tell a story.

Part of the fun is in dressing up for your performance. You will have great fun finding plenty of clothes and odds-and-ends to help you.

Here are some titles for sketches you might like to perform:

▷ The day the wind blew at camp

▷ Blue Six take off for the moon
▷ The mystery of the silent horseman
▷ Akela gets the recipe wrong

No doubt you will be able to think of some of your own.

WHY NOT TRY THE ENTERTAINER BADGE?

2. MUSIC
Take part in a performance by singing, playing a musical instrument or dancing.

Your performance can be done either on your own, or with a group of Cubs. Whichever you choose to do, you must make sure that you have practised and that you do it to the best of your ability.

WHY NOT TRY THE MUSICIAN BADGE?

*Choose at least **one** activity in Creativity*

Creativity

3. WORSHIP
Contribute to, and take part in a Scout's Own service.

A Scout's Own service may be held anywhere — at camp, on a Pack Holiday or at a Pack Meeting. Your Leader will help you to decide what you can do.

If you are at camp, you might choose a clearing in the woods in which to hold the service. Maybe your friends could follow a tracking trail which leads there. This would be a nice way of telling them that there is a special path they can follow to talk to God.

4. PUPPETS
Contribute to, and take part in a puppet or shadow play.

There are many types of puppets. Some puppets fit onto your hand like a glove, and all the movement is done by bending and wiggling your fingers. You could make dolls or cardboard cut-outs which are hung on fine string. These are worked from above.

There are others which you can make yourself out of paper, and which fit over the end of your fingers.

Other simple cut-out figures can be made from strong card

Secure paper loop to the back of finger.

Mount cut out figure onto stick — place against a screen.

and stuck onto the end of thin sticks. By placing these behind a screen made out of white paper, and shining a strong light behind them, you can make a 'shadowgraph' play to entertain your friends. This needs lots of preparation and plenty of practice.

Badge link

WHY NOT TRY THE HANDYMAN BADGE?

*Choose at least **one** activity in Creativity*

Creativity

5.REPORTERS

Contribute a story, report, poem or picture to a Group or local newsletter.

This is your chance to act as a news reporter. Write a story or a report for your Group or other local newsletter. It can be about something interesting that you have seen or done, either in the Pack or at home. If you prefer, you could write a poem about the event.

Another idea would be to take a photograph of something which is 'news' and have that printed in the newsletter.

A few of you could get together and make your own Wall Newspaper. On it you could place all your stories, reports, pictures, messages, football results, cartoons... the list is endless!

6. PAINTING AND DRAWING

Paint or draw some pictures or create a comic strip or series of cartoons.

You can draw your own designs, or paint any subject you like. You could try to make up a comic strip like you see in

comics or the papers but using your own characters.

Here is one started — see if you can finish the last two pictures.

Another good idea is to try to copy a photograph, using a pencil and a piece of white paper.

Badge link

WHY NOT TRY THE ARTIST BADGE?

*Choose at least **one** activity in Creativity*

Creativity

7. MAGIC
Perform some magic tricks.

There are a number of books available to help you learn some great magic tricks. And remember that magicians have two special rules of their own...

▷ Never perform a trick until you can do it properly at least three times in a row.

▷ Never tell the audience the secret of how a trick is done.

Try this trick to get you started:

You will need: two sheets of newspaper.

What you do: Tear a long strip off one of the sheets of newspaper about 3cm wide. Fold this backwards and forwards, concertina-style so that you end up with a package of paper measuring about 3cm × 2cm.

Tear the paper as shown below so that you have the shape of a man (and when you open the folded paper, you will have a row of men holding hands).

Hide this folded-up paper in your hand as you show your audience the other new sheet of paper. Crumple it up and tear odd pieces off it, asking the audience to help you — but be careful not to tear the prepared piece which is hiding in your hand.

When most of the paper has been torn up, the audience will not think you have done the trick properly, until you pull from your hand the paper chain of little men!

8. TAKING PICTURES
Take a set of slides or photographs or contribute to a video or film and show it to others.

With a set of photographs you should be able to show what happened at an event, such as a camp, and you should not need to write many words on your display. Make sure that they are in the right order!

A set of slides can be accompanied by a tape recorded commentary as you show them.

If you are lucky enough to have a video camera at home or in the Pack, you can help with making a video film to show to an audience.

Badge link
WHY NOT TRY THE ENTERTAINER BADGE?

Badge link

WHY NOT TRY THE PHOTOGRAPHER BADGE?

*Choose at least **one** activity in Creativity*

Creativity

9. CRAFTS

Make something using a craft method which is new to you, or make a model or kit finished to a good standard.

It could be working with paper, wood or odds-and-ends. You might try a model kit using balsa wood or plastic. You must follow the instructions very carefully and be most careful about the glue. Do not breathe in the fumes and do not get it stuck all over everything else! Be sure that an adult is with you if you need to use sharp tools.

MAKE AND FLY A KITE

You will need one lightweight plastic dustbin liner; two small garden canes; sticky tape; thin string.

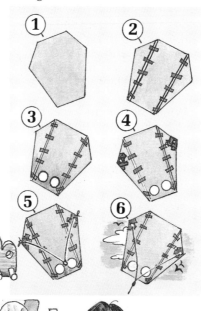

1. Cut and open out the plastic sack and cut out the shape shown.
2. Cut the garden canes to fit down the edges of the kite and tape them in position.
3. Carefully cut the two air holes.
4. Put lots of tape over the corners of the wings to strengthen them and pierce a small hole in each one.
5. Cut a length of string one and a half times the width of your kite and attach each end to the two small holes. Tie a small loop in the middle of the string.
6. Attach the ball of string to the loop and let fly!

10. OVER TO YOU

Take part in any other form of entertainment or hand-craft as agreed with a Leader.

You can take part in any other kind of entertainment or produce any other form of art or craft that is first agreed with a Leader.

Badge link

WHY NOT TRY THE CRAFTSMAN BADGE?

*Choose at least **one** activity in Creativity*

Your Community

INTRODUCTION

Everyone is part of a community – it is where you live. It is full of interesting people, places and things. By finding out more about where you live, you might be able to do something really useful in your community.

You must choose at least ONE of the six activities in this section.

1. LOCAL FEATURES
Show you know where the main features and landmarks are in your area.

Try to obtain a map of your local area. Walk around the area carefully and mark on the map important landmarks like your home, churches, fire station, police station, doctor, dentist, shops, schools, library, Pack Headquarters and so on. You should also include things like public telephones, post boxes, bus stops, railway stations and pedestrian crossings.

You might like to make your own sketch map or model of the local area and show it to your Six.

Badge link

WHY NOT TRY THE NAVIGATOR BADGE?

2. LOCAL SURVEY
Help to carry out a survey of your area such as types of transport, buildings or facilities for the elderly, the disabled or children.

PLACES	HOW THEY COULD BE IMPROVED
SWIMMING POOL	
SUPERMARKET	
POST OFFICE	
LIBRARY	
BUSES	

Can you imagine what it is like to be very old and have difficulty getting around? Or to be disabled in some way? How do parents with prams cope in getting around your community?

Does your local area look after young people of your age at all? Are there any parks, play areas or adventure playgrounds? What other services are provided by your council, local churches or organisations for children?

Take a good look at your local post office, church, doctor's surgery, building society, bank, supermarket. Are there steps, revolving doors, handrails? Are they warm or cold inside? Is it noisy or quiet? Are there any seats?

Make a chart of places or facilities used by the elderly and/or the disabled in your area. What would you do to make it easier for these people to use them?

*Choose at least **one** activity in your Community*

Your Community

3. LOCAL HISTORY

Find out about any person or event, past or present, for which your area is well known.

Ask Akela, your parents or someone who has lived in your area for a long time to tell you something about your home town. Then with a friend try to find out more details.

You might be able to borrow

some old photographs showing what your local area used to look like — you could then take some photographs of how it looks today. Show the photographs to other Cub Scouts and see if they can match up the old and the new ones.

Your area could be famous for something historical, modern, an invention, something Royal, a tradition, a personality or a sport.

What you could ask...

▷ **About a place:** Where is it? How long has it existed? Does it still exist? What is it used for now? Why is it famous? Who does it belong to? Where does its name come from?

▷ **About a person:** Who is it? Why are they famous? Where were they born? When did they die? Where are they buried? Which school did they attend? Where did they live? Are there any roads or places named after them?

▷ **About a tradition:** What is it? When did it start? What was its purpose? Is it still in existence? What happens?

Badge link

WHY NOT TRY THE LOCAL HISTORIAN BADGE?

4. LOCAL TRANSPORT

Go on a local expedition with an adult using time-tables and local transport.

Anyone going on a journey by train, bus or aeroplane will need to use a timetable. This will tell you when your journey begins and when you should arrive.

With the help of an adult, learn how to use the timetable below. Can you answer all the questions?

BESTWOOD	0620	0715	0755	0910	1050
Tipton	0630	....	0805	0925	1100
Flaxbury	0635	0730	0810	0925	1105
CUBVILLE	0640	....	0815	0930	1110
BESTWOOD	1205	1435	1620	1745	1835
Tipton	1215	1445	....	....	1845
Flaxbury	1220	1450	1635	1800	1850
CUBVILLE	1225	1455	1640	....	1855
BESTWOOD	2010	2235			
Tipton	....	2245			
Flaxbury	2025	2250			
CUBVILLE	....	2255			

1. How long does it take to travel from Bestwood to Cubville?
2. How long does it take to travel from Bestwood to Flaxbury?
3. If I leave Tipton at 1445, at what time should I arrive in Cubville.
4. If I need to get to Flaxbury by 1220, when must I leave Bestwood?
5. How many buses stop at Tipton?
6. What time does the last bus leave Bestwood?

Badge link

WHY NOT TRY THE NAVIGATOR BADGE?

*Choose at least **one** activity in your Community*

Your Community

5. LOCAL VISIT

Take part in a visit to a local place of interest and find out how it serves the community.

Your local fire, police and ambulance station all serve your community but so do radio stations, rubbish disposal plants, newspaper offices and telephone exchanges.

Someone will need to get permission for you to visit any of these places. If you do go to one, find out as much as you can about the work involved, the services offered and the people who work there.

Badge link

WHY NOT TRY THE COMMUNITY BADGE?

6. LOCAL PEOPLE

Meet or visit someone who lives or works in your area and find out what he or she does to help the community.

Make a list of people who help the community. For example: nurses, milkmen, bank managers, road sweepers.

Choose one from your list and say what they do for your community and how you might manage without them.

Talk to one of the people on your list and ask them about their job.

Lots of people help the community by joining one of the many national or local organisations set up to help others. Are there any in your area? Is there any way you, as a Cub Scout, can help them? Akela may invite someone to come and tell you about one of these organisations.

Think of three ways you could help.

MY LIST OF PEOPLE WHO HELP THE COMMUNITY	
1	5
2	6
3	7
4	8

*Choose at least **one** activity in your Community*

Countries and Cultures

INTRODUCTION

In the United Kingdom there are lots of people who have different customs and traditions. This part of your Award will give you the chance to discover some of them.

You must choose at least ONE of the four activities in this section.

1. CUSTOMS AND TRADITIONS
Find out something about customs, traditions or crafts that are special to your area, religion or culture and share it with your Pack.

You may be able to find out about some local traditions or crafts where you live which you can describe to other Cub Scouts.

You could visit a local craftsman or someone who knows a lot about traditions in your area. You could talk to a neighbour from a different culture about their religion and customs.

You may find out more at a local museum, craft shop or library.

Badge link

WHY NOT TRY THE MY FAITH BADGE?

2. ROYAL FAMILY
Know the first verse of the National Anthem and how to behave when it is played and find out something that interests you about the way of life of the Royal Family.

God save our gracious Queen,
Long live our noble Queen,
God save the Queen!
Send her victorious,
Happy and glorious,
Long to reign over us,
God save the Queen!

When you go to special events or gatherings, you may hear the National Anthem played. It is important that you stand quietly at the Alert as it is a way in which we show respect for the Queen and the country in which we live.

Find out something that interests you about the members of the Royal Family, such as their hobbies and sports. What car do they ride in? What countries have they visited recently?

Make a Royal Family scrap book with pictures or drawings.

*Choose at least **one** activity from Countries and Cultures.*

Countries and Cultures

3. FLAGS AND SAINTS

Know the flags that make up the Union Flag and how to prepare it for flagbreak. Know the stories of the Patron Saints of the United Kingdom and some of the emblems and traditions associated with them.

The United Kingdom has its own National flag. It is made up of three different flags.

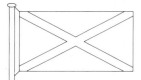

The old Irish Flag
The cross of St. Patrick, the Irish Saint

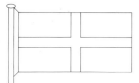

The English Flag
The cross of St George

The Scottish Flag
Showing the diagonal cross on which St. Andrew was crucified.

Can you find out the correct colours of all these flags and colour them in.

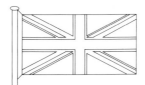

The three flags were put together to make the Union Flag.

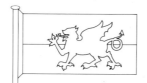

The Welsh Flag is not a cross and could not be used in the Union Flag. Can you find out the colours of it?

THE SAINTS AND THEIR COUNTRIES

St. David of Wales – Saint Day March 1st

St. Patrick of Ireland – Saint Day March 17th

St. George of England – Saint Day April 23rd

St. Andrew of Scotland – Saint Day November 30th

4. NATIONAL CHARITY

Find out about an organisation that helps those in need in this country and do something to support it.

In your local area there may be many charities. Do you know what they actually do?

Ask Akela if you can write to a charity which sounds interesting to you. You could ask them to send you some posters and leaflets about their organisation. Where could you put these to help tell people

about what the organisation does and what help it needs from the public?

Your Leader might agree to let you invite someone from the charity to come and talk to the Pack.

Can you offer help to support the charity in any way?

WHY NOT TRY THE COMMUNITY BADGE?

THE ADVENTURE AWARD

*Choose at least **one** activity from Countries and Cultures.*

49

My Promise

INTRODUCTION

Do you remember the day that you were invested and made your Promise to Akela in front of the Pack? It is not always easy to keep that Promise, but we have to keep trying all the time. This section will help to remind you how important it is.

You must complete BOTH parts of this section.

1. Make a prayer poster, chart or collage

Think of all the things you enjoy. Try to find some pictures of your favourite things. It could be food, toys, people or animals. Either cut out the pictures from old magazines or draw pictures to make a poster. Under each picture write a short prayer to say thank you to God for giving you these things.

It may be fairly easy to think of the things you like, but now try to think of all the things you are sorry about. Maybe you ignored a job you were supposed to do, like tidying your room or cleaning out the hamster's cage. Perhaps you have been unkind to someone.

Dear God, thank you for ....
....
....

Dear God, I am sorry for ....
....
....

Draw some pictures, or make a chart like the one above, asking God to forgive you for the wrong things you have said, thought or done.

2. When you have finished most of this award, talk to a Leader about how you have tried to put your Promise and Law into practice in everything you have done.

Look back at the activities you have done so far in the Adventure Award. Choose four activities where you think you have done your best, and fill in your list in the spaces provided.

Now show these to a Leader and talk about all the things you have tried to do to keep your Cub Scout Promise.

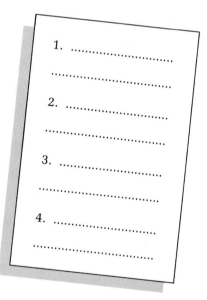

1. ....
2. ....
3. ....
4. ....

Badge link

WHY NOT TRY THE MY FAITH BADGE?

*Complete **both** activities in My Promise.*

Scout Family Badge

INTRODUCTION

As soon as you complete these TWO activities you will receive a Scout Family Badge to wear on your uniform.

1. Find out what type of activities Scouts do and some of the badges and awards that they wear.

If you were a Scouting detective and you looked at a Scout uniform you would be able to tell something about the Scout by 'reading' his badges.

Meet a Scout: Invite a Scout to visit your Pack and tell you about his badges and awards.

What activities do Scouts do?

What do Scouts do to gain their badges and awards?

2. Take part in a District or County event or join in an activity with Beaver Scouts, Scouts or Venture Scouts.

Do other Packs in your District or County/Area have different scarves from you?

How many different scarves have you seen? Draw the ones you can remember on a large sheet of paper and write down the name of Groups to which they belong.

ADVENTURE AWARD
THIS IS TO CERTIFY

NAME ....

OF THE ....

has completed the Adventure Award

SIGNED .... AKELA

DATE ....

*Complete **both** activities for the Scout Family Badge.*

Adventure Crest Award

The Adventure Crest Award is the highest Award you can gain as a Cub Scout. You will have a lot of fun while you are doing the activities and will get a smart badge to wear on your uniform when you have finished it to show everyone that you like an adventure.

You must complete each section of this Award.

TICK WHEN COMPLETED:

▷ **OUTDOOR SCOUTING**
Choose at least FOUR activities

▷ **SPORTS AND HOBBIES**
Complete BOTH parts

▷ **HELPING OTHERS**
Choose at least TWO activities

▷ **LOOKING AFTER YOURSELF**
Choose at least TWO activities

▷ **SCIENCE AND NATURE**
Choose at least ONE from science and at least ONE from nature

▷ **CREATIVITY**
Choose at least ONE activity

▷ **YOUR COMMUNITY**
Choose at least ONE activity

▷ **COUNTRIES AND CULTURES**
Choose at least ONE activity

▷ **MY PROMISE**
Complete BOTH parts

▷ **SCOUT FAMILY BADGE**
Complete BOTH parts

Remember...
The Scout Family Badge

Adventure Crest Award

OUTDOOR SCOUTING

You must choose at least FOUR activities from this section.

1. MAPPING ☐
2. FIRE LIGHTING ☐
3. KNOTS ☐
4. COMPASS ☐
5. HIKING EXPEDITION ☐
6. SHELTER BUILDING ☐
7. CAMPING ☐
8. CAMP GADGETS ☐

SPORTS AND HOBBIES

You must complete BOTH parts in this section

1. SPORTSMANLIKE ATTITUDE ☐
2. CHOOSE TWO SPORTS OR HOBBIES ☐

HELPING OTHERS

You must choose at least TWO activities from this section.

1. FIRST AID ☐
2. WATER SAFETY ☐
3. HOME SAFETY ☐
4. SPECIAL GOOD TURNS ☐
5. HELPING AKELA ☐

LOOKING AFTER YOURSELF

You must choose at least TWO activities from this section.

1. KEEPING HEALTHY ☐
2. KEEPING FIT ☐
3. GOOD FOOD ☐
4. ROAD SAFETY ☐

SCIENCE AND NATURE

You must choose at least ONE from SCIENCE and ONE from NATURE.

SCIENCE

1. WEATHER STATION ☐
2. MAINTENANCE ☐
3. WORKING MODELS ☐
4. CONSTRUCTION KITS ☐
5. TECHNICAL EQUIPMENT ☐

NATURE

1. SURVEYS ☐
2. CONSERVATION PROJECT ☐
3. WILDLIFE IN DANGER ☐
4. FEED THE BIRDS ☐
5. ADOPT A PLOT ☐

CREATIVITY

You must choose at least ONE activity from this section which you did not choose for your Adventure Award.

1. ACTING ☐
2. MUSIC ☐
3. WORSHIP ☐
4. PUPPETS ☐
5. REPORTERS ☐
6. PAINTING & DRAWING ☐
7. MAGIC ☐
8. TAKING PICTURES ☐
9. CRAFTS ☐
10. OVER TO YOU ☐

YOUR COMMUNITY

You must choose at least ONE acitivity from this section.

1. COMMUNITY HELP ☐
2. COMMUNITY GROUPS ☐
3. COMMUNITY PROJECT ☐
4. PEOPLE WHO HELP ☐
5. LOCAL CHARITY ☐

COUNTRIES AND CULTURES

You must choose at least ONE activity from this section.

1. INTERNATIONAL MEETING ☐
2. INTERNATIONAL ORGANISATIONS ☐
3. INTERNATIONAL SCOUTING ☐
4. OTHER PEOPLE'S CULTURE ☐

MY PROMISE

You must complete BOTH parts in this section.

1. MAKE A PRAYER ☐
2. TALK WITH LEADER ☐

SCOUT FAMILY BADGE

You must complete BOTH parts in this section.

1. FIND OUT ABOUT THE SCOUT PATROL SYSTEM ☐
2. AN ACTIVITY WITH SCOUTS ☐

53

Outdoor Scouting

INTRODUCTION

Here is a chance for you to learn some Scouting skills, or perhaps to get better at some you already know.

You must choose at least FOUR of the eight activities in this section.

1. MAPPING
Use an Ordnance Survey map to plan a journey or hike.

If you are going on a journey, you will need a map to show you the way. Make sure you know what the different coloured lines mean — after all, you wouldn't want to plan a hike along a motorway or river!

To help you remember your route, fold the map so you can see all of your route and put it into a clear plastic bag. Clip this very tightly in place with bulldog clips or sticky tape. You will now be able to draw your route on the plastic, using a waterproof ink felt-tipped pen.

When planning your route, remember to...

▷ Avoid marshy areas.
  ▷ Keep to roads or footpaths.

▷ Measure the distance you plan to walk (the scale printed on the map will help you to do this).
▷ Work out how long it will take you (the normal speed is about six kilometres an hour).
▷ Allow enough time for walking over rough ground and hills, which will slow you down and make you more tired.

▷ Allow time for a lunch break and for sightseeing.

Look at the contour lines (the thin brown lines which show the height of the land above sea level) as they will show you how steep a hill is. It is best to walk along a route between the lines rather than crossing over the lines.

Badge link

WHY NOT TRY THE MAP READER BADGE?

*Choose at least **four** activities in Outdoor Scouting.*

Outdoor Scouting

2. FIRE LIGHTING
Light a fire out of doors and cook something on it.

Before you start this activity, remember when lighting a fire you should have an adult nearby, just in case the fire gets out of control.

Remember not to cook on the flames. Wait until they have died down and you are left with glowing embers. You are then ready to cook....

Don't forget to put the fire out once you have finished cooking. Replace the turf and make sure the whole area is as tidy as when you came.

1. *Collect plenty of dry, dead wood and find a clear patch of ground. (Be careful not to damage grass or trees.)*

2. *Place some bricks round the area.*

3. *Place a ball of dry tinder (dead grass, paper and so on) in the centre.*

4. *Lean some very thin sticks against the ball to form a pyramid.*

5. *Light the tinder with a match and keep feeding the fire with thin sticks.*

6. *Once the thin sticks are alight, gradually feed thicker twigs on the fire. Keep feeding it regularly.*

7. *You could cook sausages, beef-burgers, apples or beans in tin foil or put a grill over the fire and use a billy can to cook something. Make sure that you put the fire out completely when you have finished.*

Badge link

WHY NOT TRY THE EXPLORER BADGE?

*Choose at least **four** activities in Outdoor Scouting.*

Outdoor Scouting

ADVENTURE CREST AWARD

3. KNOTS

Learn how to tie at least three knots which are new to you and use them in an activity, if possible out of doors.

Here are some examples...

ROUND TURN AND TWO HALF-HITCHES

This knot is often used for tying boats to their mooring posts.

BOWLINE

This knot is used in rock climbing, because it is very strong and will not slip. It is also known as the rescue knot.

PARCEL KNOT

This knot is for tying up parcels securely.

HIGHWAYMAN'S HITCH

This is a clever knot, used to tie horses' reins to a post and is easy to release.

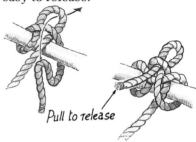

Pull to release

Badge link

WHY NOT TRY THE CAMPER BADGE?

4. COMPASS

Use a Silva-type compass in an outdoor activity.

A Silva compass looks like the one shown here. It is very useful because it divides the compass up into 360 points (or 'degrees'), rather than just North, South, East and West. You can therefore find your way to a given point very accurately.

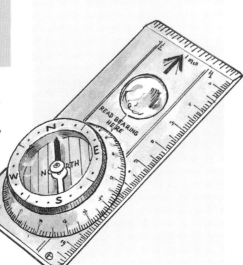

READ BEARING HERE

When you have learned to use the compass, you could lay a secret trail for a friend in a park or back garden. You will need to give him a number of compass bearings to follow — but you will have to work them out carefully first.

Badge link

WHY NOT TRY THE NAVIGATOR BADGE?

*Choose at least **four** activities in Outdoor Scouting.*

Outdoor Scouting

5. HIKING EXPEDITION

With a Leader, help to plan and take part in a hiking expedition with other Cub Scouts.

When you plan a hiking expedition, you have to make sure that you are well prepared for it. You can not just put on a coat and walk up the road for a few miles or you may get lost, hungry or just bored. A Leader will help you plan your expedition with other Cub Scouts, and will make sure that you are properly prepared.

Where will you go?
▷ A hike in the country along a footpath?
▷ A hike to a local castle, cathedral, or stately home?
▷ A hike along a river?
▷ A hike to an ancient ruin?
▷ A hike to a swimming pool, lake or activity centre?

When will you go?
▷ Make sure everybody is free to go on the expedition.
▷ Make sure that wherever you plan to go will be open on the day you choose.

What will you need to take with you?

1.....................
2..................... 6 ....
3..................... 7 ....
4..................... 8 ....
5..................... 9 ....
10 ....

How will you get to the starting point of the hike?
▷ By car?   ▷ By train?
▷ ....

How much will it cost?
▷ Entrance fees: ▷ Travel:
▷ ....

Badge link

WHY NOT TRY THE EXPLORER BADGE?

*Choose at least **four** activities in Outdoor Scouting.*

6. SHELTER BUILDING
Build a shelter out of doors.

Shelters can have all sorts of names, such as dens or bivouacs. Make sure you have the permission of the land-owner before you build your own shelter, and never pull live branches off trees to make it.

7. CAMPING
Spend at least one night in a tent with other Cub Scouts.

You may be able to go away for one or more nights with Cub Scouts on a camp, either with your own Pack or on a District or County/Area camp.

Make sure you know how to behave in a tent so that you and your friends will get a good night's sleep.

RULES OF OUR TENT
1. Shoes to be taken off out-side tent.
2. Don't touch sides of tent.
3. No food allowed in tent.
4. No bundling in and out of tent.
5. Lights out at 10 p.m.
6. No talking after lights out.
7. No one outside tent after lights out except to go to the loo.

Badge link

WHY NOT TRY THE CAMPER BADGE?

*Choose at least **four** activities in Outdoor Scouting.*

Outdoor Scouting

8. CAMP GADGETS
Design and make at least two gadgets you could use on camp.

Here are three useful gadgets — perhaps you could invent your own?

You could make camp gadgets out of garden canes or sticks. They can be joined together with string, rope or rubber bands. Gadget making will give you a chance to practice your knotting and camp craft skills. Remember the Country Code, don't cut or damage living trees or bushes. Use only dead but strong wood. Always remember to leave the site as you found it!

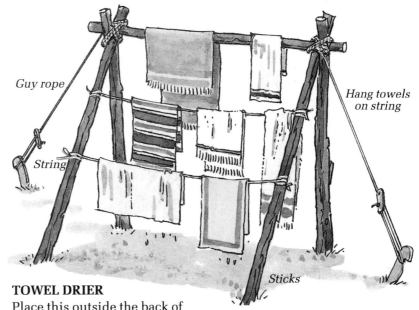

Guy rope

String

Hang towels on string

Sticks

TOWEL DRIER
Place this outside the back of your tent where the sun and wind can dry your towels and flannels.

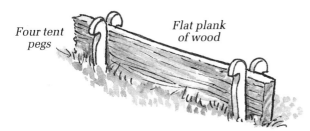

Four tent pegs

Flat plank of wood

SHOE SCRAPER
Put this in front of the tent so that you can clean the mud off your shoes before you take them off to go into the tent.

BOWL STAND
Place this outside your tent or camp toilet so that you can wash your hands when necessary.

*Choose at least **four** activities in Outdoor Scouting.*

Sports and Hobbies

INTRODUCTION

This is your opportunity to share with your friends your knowledge and skills in a sport or hobby, and to try a new one.

You must complete BOTH parts of this section.

1. Show a sportsmanlike attitude in all Pack games and activities and know why this is important.

2. Choose at least two sports or hobbies. Choose ONE which you already do and tell other Cub Scouts and Leaders what you have done recently to improve or develop your hobby or sport – and try ONE which is new to you.

Do the Cub Scouts in your Six still say things like:

> *'You cheated'*   *'It's not fair'*
> *'It's your fault'*   *'Clumsy'*
> *'You let us down'*   *'Stupid'*

...or have you helped them to show a sportsmanlike attitude?

We all need to work together as a team. It helps the team if everyone feels needed and has a part to play. It is important to say thank you.

Look at the list of sports and hobbies back on page 32.

If you have already done the Adventure Award you must choose another two different Sports or Hobbies. Choose one sport or hobby that you already enjoy and share your chosen sport or hobby with other Cub Scouts and Leaders.

You might like to tell them –
▷ How long you have been doing this sport or hobby
▷ Where you go to do it
▷ What you actually do
▷ How you do it
▷ What materials, equipment or kit you use
▷ Who helps you
▷ What you have done to improve or develop your sport or hobby recently

Show examples or photographs of your sport or hobby.

Now choose a sport or hobby that is new to you and take part in it for a few weeks.
▷ Did you enjoy this new sport or hobby?
▷ What did you like most about it?
▷ Have you shared this sport or hobby with a friend?
▷ How often have you taken part in this new sport or hobby?
▷ Are you doing better now than when you first started?
▷ Are you going to continue with this new sport or hobby?

Badge link

WHY NOT TRY THE HOBBIES OR SPORTSMAN BADGES?

*Complete **both** parts of Sports and Hobbies.*

Helping Others

INTRODUCTION

When you were invested as a Cub Scout, you made a Promise to help other people. In this section you have the chance to make a special effort to help others.

You must choose at least TWO of the five activities from this section.

1. FIRST AID
Show you know how to stop bleeding by using direct pressure and show two uses of a triangular bandage.

BLEEDING
If someone cuts themself it is very important to try to stop the bleeding because if he loses too much blood, he will become

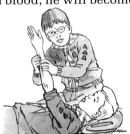

very ill. Always remember to try and get an adult to help you whenever you can, but as a Cub Scout you should be prepared to try and stop the bleeding yourself.

To control bleeding you must do the following:
▷ Immediately apply direct pressure with your fingers or palm of hand.
▷ If the wound is large, squeeze the edges together with your fingers.
▷ Lay the patient down.
▷ If the wound is on a leg or arm raise the limb so that the blood flow slows down.

▷ Apply a sterile dressing tied firmly but not too tight.
▷ If bleeding still continues, do not remove the first dressing, but put another one on top.
▷ Get the patient to hospital.

TRIANGULAR BANDAGES
A triangular bandage is a special type of bandage which is used to give an injury support, such as a broken arm or crushed hand.

Your Leader will show you the correct way to apply these

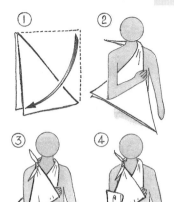

bandages and maybe someone from the St John Ambulance, St. Andrews or the British Red Cross could come to a Pack Meeting to give you a demonstration.

WHY NOT TRY THE FIRST AID BADGE?

*Choose at least **two** activities from Helping Others.*

Helping Others

ADVENTURE CREST AWARD

2. WATER SAFETY

Know the water safety rules and show you can use some rescue skills to help someone who has fallen in the water.

With a Leader or another adult, visit your local swimming pool and ask if you can use the pool to practise your rescue skills. You could practise rescue skills from the side of a swimming pool or even on dry land.

Remember the Water Code — and try to get adult help if there is nothing you can do to help someone in difficulty without putting yourself in danger.

To help someone who has fallen in the water, you should...

REACH

▷ Look for something to help pull him out: a stick, rope or piece of clothing.
▷ Lie down to prevent yourself being pulled in.

THROW

▷ If you cannot reach the person, throw a floating object such as a football or plastic bottle, for them to hold onto.

WADE

▷ If the water is shallow enough, you might be able to walk closer to the person. Never go out of your depth and do not try to swim to him or you may get into difficulties yourself. If possible, hold on to someone or something on the bank.

ROW

▷ If you are in a boat, you could help pull the person aboard. Remember to pull him in at the stern (the back) of the boat and not the side — or the boat might turn over and you may fall in too.

Try to improve your water safety skills:

▷ Float on your back in the swimming pool for as long as you can.
▷ Tread water.
▷ Climb out of the deep end.
▷ Help someone else out from the deep end.
▷ Throw a float to someone accurately.

Badge link

WHY NOT TRY THE SWIMMER BADGE?

*Choose at least **two** activities from Helping Others.*

Helping Others

3. HOME SAFETY

Know what you can do to prevent crime and accidents in the home and know what to do in cases of emergencies at home or in your Scout Headquarters.

This is a picture of someone's house. The owner has gone away on holiday and left the house empty.

Mark the things that would make it easy for a burglar to know the house was empty and the ways he could break in.

Collect some information from the local Police Crime Prevention Officer and make a poster or collage about your home or Headquarters on how

and why we should prevent crime.

If there was a fire in your home or Headquarters you should always know what to do.

Make an emergency drill poster for your home or Headquarters. For example:

EMERGENCY DRILL
▷ **Don't panic**
▷ **Listen**
▷ **Leave Quietly**
▷ **Walk**
▷ **Assemble in a given place**
▷ **Check that everyone is present**
▷ **Dial 999**

With Akela make a checklist of your Headquarters to see if it is a safe place. Here are some ideas to help you:
▷ How many exits are there?
▷ Are any emergency lights working?
▷ Are the exits clear?
▷ How many fire extinguishers are there...?
▷ When were they last tested?
▷ How many times a year do you practise a fire drill?

Badge link

WHY NOT TRY THE HOME SAFETY BADGE

*Choose at least **two** activities from Helping Others.*

Helping Others

4. SPECIAL GOOD TURNS
Take a leading part in a Pack or Six good turn.

A Cub Scout does a good turn every day. This can usually be something small like clearing up after a meal, opening a door for someone in a shop or carrying a bag for somebody. Sometimes it is nice to do a special good turn.

For example:
▷ Help clear rubbish from a local green or patch of ground.
▷ With your Six, arrange to plant some bulbs for the local community.
▷ Visit an old people's home to help out or do some entertaining.
▷ Collect used tin foil, stamps and so on for local charities which sell them for recycling.
▷ Collect old magazines and toys for local hospitals.

5. HELPING AKELA
Take on a job in the life of your Pack for at least four weeks.

The Leaders in your Pack are always very busy planning the meetings and activities for you. Offer to help Akela by doing something special for a period of not less than four weeks, such as:
▷ Help Akela to do the attendance register
▷ Help a new Cub Scout learn something he finds difficult
▷ Keep the cupboards tidy
▷ Look after the games equipment
▷ Help run some games.
▷ Prepare the flag for flagbreak each week

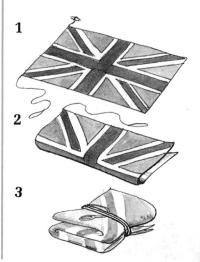

*Choose at least **two** activities from Helping Others.*

Looking after Yourself

INTRODUCTION

Cub Scouts learn to take care of themselves and others. This shows that you are getting older and able to look after yourself more.

You must choose at least TWO of the four activities in this section.

1. KEEPING HEALTHY

Show that you know about personal hygiene and cleanliness.

Your skin is an important part of you which keeps growing all through your life. You can help by keeping it clean. Tick off this list:

Are you a clean person?
Do you...

Wash your hands before eating?
Keep your finger nails clean and cut short?
Wash your hands and face before going to bed?
Wash your hands after going to the toilet?
Clean your teeth every day?
Visit your dentist?
Have a bath or shower regularly?
Know how often to change your clothes?

...and do you know why you need to do these things?

Badge link

WHY NOT TRY THE HEALTH AND FITNESS BADGE?

2. KEEPING FIT

Show that you know how to keep yourself fit and what can damage your health.

You should always try to keep fit and healthy. You have a brain to help you think and a body which can move.

Cross out the things shown which will not help the brain and body to keep fit and healthy.

RECORD OF KEEP FIT ACTIVITIES

	SUN	MON	TUE	WED	THU	FRI	SAT
JOGGING							
SIT UPS							
PRESS UPS							
BUNNY JUMPS							

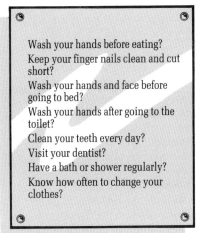

*Choose at least **two** activities from Looking After Yourself.*

Looking after Yourself

3. GOOD FOOD
Show that you know which foods are better for you and the dangers of a poor diet.

Your food helps you:
▷ to move and keep warm
▷ to grow

▷ to repair damaged bones and skin.

Take a look through some magazines and cut out some pictures of food. Now arrange them into three groups, things you should eat often, things you should eat from time to time and things you should keep as special treats. Stick them onto a piece of paper and talk to someone else about why you have put them in each particular group.

4. ROAD SAFETY
Identify at least ten traffic signs and either show you know how to cycle safely or know how to behave safely as a car passenger.

Here are some road signs. Do you know what they mean? Remember, when you are using the road you do not have a lot of time to think about their meaning so you will be safer if you can recognise them really quickly.

There are not many places which are just for cyclists alone, so you need to be very careful when you are out on your bicycle. You can learn to become a safer cyclist in lots of different ways. One of the best ways is to take the National Cycling Proficiency Test when you are old enough. Courses for this are held in a variety of places so you would need to find the one nearest to you.

When you are a passenger in a car, you must remember not to disturb the driver or you may have an accident.

In the box below, write down how you should behave in a car, showing things you should and should not do...

SHOULD	SHOULD NOT

WHY NOT TRY THE CYCLIST BADGE?

*Choose at least **two** activities from Looking After Yourself.*

Science and Nature

INTRODUCTION

The world of science and nature is very exciting as it is changing every day. This section will help you to find out more about what is happening in the world around you.

You must choose at least ONE of the five in SCIENCE and at least ONE of the five in NATURE.

Science

Choose ONE in SCIENCE

1. WEATHER STATION
Set up a weather station with at least 3 different instruments and use it to record the weather for 2 weeks.

Everybody talks about the weather. Set up your own weather station to keep a record of the weather — you could even try making your own weather forecast.

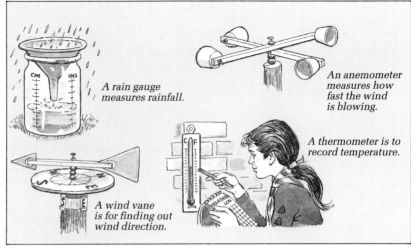

A rain gauge measures rainfall.

An anemometer measures how fast the wind is blowing.

A thermometer is to record temperature.

A wind vane is for finding out wind direction.

WEATHER LOG

TIME													
DAY	S	M	T	W	T	F	S	S	M	T	W	T	S
WIND DIRECTION													
WIND SPEED													
HUMIDITY													
RAINFALL													
TEMPERATURE													
CLOUD TYPE													

A thermometer is used for measuring temperature. Learn how to use one. Place the thermometer in a shaded place.

Keep a record of the temperature by reading the thermometer at the same time each day.

CLOUD TYPES

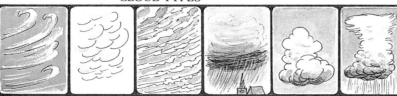

Cirrus   *Altocumulus*   *Nimbostratus*   *Stratus*   *Cumulus*   *Cumulonimbus*

Badge link

WHY NOT TRY THE SCIENTIST BADGE?

Science and Nature

2. MAINTENANCE

Help an adult with the routine maintenance of a bicycle, car, model railway or other machinery.

Regular maintenance of any machinery is very important, as it means that the object will last longer and run more smoothly.

Machinery can be very dangerous — it is important not to play with or near to machinery. You should always have an adult to help you and to check what you have done.

There may be other machinery you can help maintain but always ask an adult for permission before trying anything. Always use the correct tools and be very careful.

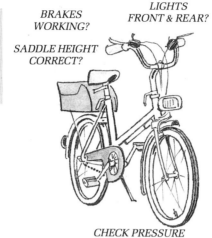

BRAKES WORKING?

LIGHTS FRONT & REAR?

SADDLE HEIGHT CORRECT?

CHECK PRESSURE AND CONDITION OF TYRES?

BICYCLE MAINTENANCE

CHECKLIST	WHAT TO NOTICE	WHAT TO DO
Spin your front wheel	*Does it wobble?*	
Spin your pedals	*Are they loose?*	
Check the steering	*Is it loose?*	
Move the chain up and down	*Moves more than 2cm?*	
Test the brakes	*Are they loose or worn?*	
Check your tyres	*Are they worn? Is pressure correct?*	

learn to check tyre pressure

learn to check tread on tyres

learn to check water level

learn to fill windscreen washer

learn to check oil level

*Choose at least **one** from Science.*

Science and Nature

3. WORKING MODELS

Design and make a model with some moving parts, using the correct tools and materials.

First of all decide what you are going to make and then design it.

Next collect all the appropriate materials and tools for your working model.

Now you can begin.

When you have finished — make sure you don't leave any mess.

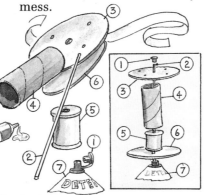

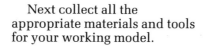

Badge link

WHY NOT TRY THE HANDYMAN BADGE?

4. CONSTRUCTION KIT

Build a model using a technical construction kit and explain how the model works.

Decide what type of model you are going to construct. It might be something to do with transport.

You might design and construct a building of the future, a model to explain the Green Cross Code to a friend, or a robot from another planet.

Once you have made your model, explain to Akela or your Six how it works and what it is supposed to do.

Badge link

WHY NOT TRY THE CRAFTSMAN BADGE?

*Choose at least **one** from Science.*

Science and Nature

5. TECHNICAL EQUIPMENT

Show you can use a computer, video camera, electronic keyboard or other piece of technical equipment, and that you know how to work its main features.

Our modern world is full of electronic gadgets. You might have a:

calculator

microwave oven

electronic keyboard

automatic camera

Demonstrate your favourite gadget, and show something you have learned recently.

hi-fi

computer

word processor

Badge link

WHY NOT TRY THE COMPUTER BADGE?

*Choose at least **one** from Science.*

Science and Nature

Nature

Choose ONE in NATURE

1. SURVEYS
Take an active part in a hedge, pond or stream survey.

A survey is a chance to look closely at the things living and growing around hedges, ponds and streams — places we often tend to ignore.

You can use books to find out the names of the animals, fish, insects or plants that you find.

You can draw or write about the different things that you discover. Perhaps you could take some photographs and put them in a scrap book?

Did you find anything unusual?

Did you find anything damaged by man?

Is there anything you can do to help improve the area?

Pond-dipping is a good way of finding out about life in a pond or stream. Gently drag a net through different areas of the pond. Make notes on what you find. Put anything interesting into a jam jar to look at it more closely. Don't forget to put everything back into the pond when you have finished. It is a good idea to wear your wellingtons for pond surveys and you should have an adult with you.

*Choose at least **one** from Nature.*

Science and Nature

2. CONSERVATION PROJECT

Take an active part in a project that helps improve the environment.

Think about how you affect your own environment.

▷ Where does your food come from?

▷ What happens to your rubbish?

▷ What animals and plants live around you?

Anything you do to your environment will have an effect on you, as well as on every other living thing sharing the environment with you.

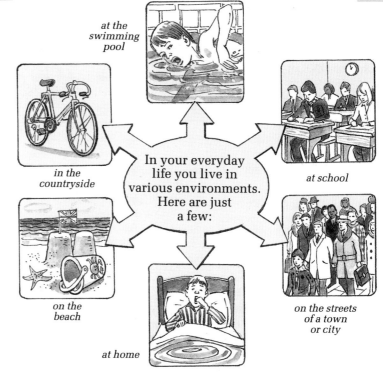

at the swimming pool

in the countryside

at school

on the beach

at home

on the streets of a town or city

In your everyday life you live in various environments. Here are just a few:

Sometimes the environment gets in a mess because it is not looked after properly. Sometimes it gets in a mess because people have been careless or thoughtless, leaving litter, pollution and graffiti on walls.

You can help your Leaders and other boys in the Pack to put things right again. Conservation means keeping our environment safe for the future. Here are some ideas:

▷ Help plant bulbs, trees or shrubs.

▷ Save newspapers for recycling.

▷ Clear a local pond or stream.

▷ Clear litter from an area.

▷ Create a pocket park on derelict ground or wasteland.

▷ Create a miniature nature reserve on derelict ground or wasteland.

▷ Collect old bottles for your local bottle bank.

Badge link

WHY NOT TRY THE WORLD CONSERVATION BADGE?

*Choose at least **one** from Nature.*

Science and Nature

3. WILDLIFE IN DANGER
Find out and display some information about the habitat and special needs of an endangered species.

In the natural world there is a fragile balance in plant and animal populations. The world's human population is growing fast and, together with danger caused by man, is putting a lot of pressure on the world's wildlife and habitats. A habitat is the natural home of a group of plants and animals, such as a pond, wood, hedgerow, sea.

Some animals are in danger of becoming extinct, which means they may disappear from the world for ever.

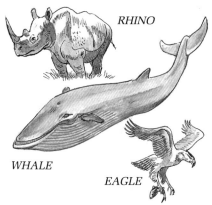

RHINO

WHALE

EAGLE

Choose any animal which is being threatened and collect or draw pictures and find out about its natural habitat. Share your findings with other Cub Scouts in the Pack.

4. FEED THE BIRDS
Make a bird feeder or table and feed the birds regularly with suitable foods.

bird table

bird feeder

old washing up liquid bottle

fill with seed

doweling perch

hole for birds to peck

▷ Bird cake made with dripping
▷ Bread
▷ Water

You may only need to feed the birds in winter. The rest of the time they should be able to find their own food and drink.

Here are some of the things birds like:
▷ Seeds
▷ Peanuts on a string
▷ Coconut
▷ Shelled peanuts hung in a bag
▷ Bacon rind

Badge link

WHY NOT TRY THE NATURALIST BADGE?

*Choose at least **one** from Nature.*

Science and Nature

5. ADOPT A PLOT
Improve and maintain a part of a garden or other piece of land.

Try to find part of a garden or allotment or derelict wasteland which needs improving and looking after. If it is a large plot you may wish to work with other Cub Scouts and Leaders.

Clear the ground of all rubbish, bricks and rubble. You will then need to prepare the soil by digging it up, especially where it is packed hard.

You could make a small nature reserve by planting seeds from different types of grass and wild flowers. If you are tidying up a garden you could just put in some young plants.

After everything is planted, you should keep working at the site. It will need to be maintained for quite some time, keeping it free of weeds and rubbish and protecting the young plants. All this hard work will certainly be worthwhile.

Badge link

WHY NOT TRY THE GARDENER BADGE?

*Choose at least **one** from Nature.*

Creativity

INTRODUCTION

The activities open to you here are exactly the same as for the Adventure Award but now you are able to choose another activity — you should try something that you have not had a chance to try before.

You must choose at least ONE of the ten activities in this section, but NOT the same activity which you chose for the Adventure Award.

1. ACTING
Contribute to and take part in a sketch or mime.

2. MUSIC
Take part in a performance by singing, playing a musical instrument or dancing.

3. WORSHIP
Contribute to and take part in a Scouts' Own Service.

4. PUPPETS
Contribute to or take part in a puppet or shadow play.

5. REPORTERS
Contribute a story, report, poem or picture to a Group or Pack Newsletter.

6. PAINTING AND DRAWING
Paint or draw some pictures or create a comic strip or series of cartoons.

7. MAGIC
Perform some magic tricks.

8. TAKING PICTURES
Take a set of slides or photographs, or contribute to a video or film and show it to others.

9. CRAFTS
Make something using a craft method which is new to you or make a model or kit finished to a good standard.

10. OVER TO YOU
Take part in any form of entertainment or handcraft as agreed with a Leader.

Full details of how you might set about your chosen activity are included in the pages dealing with the Adventure Award (see pages 40 to 44). Here are a few more ideas which you might like to try — although you may prefer to try out your own ideas.

ACTING

Acting is best done in small groups. Words should be learned carefully. It only needs one person to forget his lines and the whole thing can be spoiled.

You can practice miming by standing in front of a mirror and watching yourself at work.

PSST! ...OR NOT TO BE!

Badge link

WHY NOT TRY THE ENTERTAINER BADGE?

*Choose at least **one** activity from Creativity.*

Creativity

MUSIC

You may take part in a musical performance as part of a choir at church or school, or perhaps you are going to be in a local show or pantomime. If you want this performance to count towards your award, you will need to make sure that Akela knows about it before you start.

WHY NOT TRY THE MUSICIAN BADGE?

PAINTING AND DRAWING

You can produce some very bright and exciting designs using poster paints without ever touching a brush.

Small pieces of sponge or foam rubber can be used to dab paint onto your paper. Using this method it is quite easy to fill a very large sheet of paper very quickly, and to use several colours at the same time.

The edge of a ruler or small piece of hardboard can be dipped into the paint to give you straight lines.

WHY NOT TRY THE ARTIST BADGE?

MAGIC

The real secret of magic is for your audience to see or hear things which confuse them. Try the matchbox shaking trick.

You have on display three empty matchboxes. You pretend that one of them has a coin in it and when you pick it up and shake it, the audience will hear the coin rattling.

The secret is that inside one of your sleeves you have fastened a matchbox containing a coin which will rattle when you shake that arm.

Shake two empty boxes and replace them on the table. Shake the 'full' box with the other hand and replace that one also. Invite a member of the audience to watch you move the three boxes about and then ask him to point out the one with the coin in. He will watch very carefully as you exchange the boxes, and he will be very surprised to find that he is wrong!

*Choose at least **one** activity from Creativity.*

Creativity

TAKING PICTURES

You might like to make a great quiz for your friends using a camera.

Using the camera, take some photographs of everyday objects but from an unusual angle or just photographing part of the object. When the pictures are developed, show them to your friends and see if they can guess what the objects are. You could photograph...

▷ the spokes of a bicycle
  ▷ the wall of a building
    ▷ a bush
      ▷ a fence

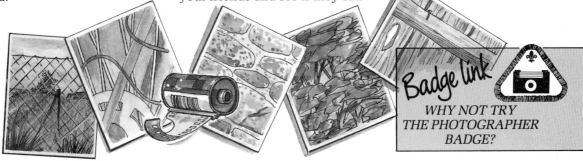

Badge link

WHY NOT TRY
THE PHOTOGRAPHER
BADGE?

CRAFTS

What craft are you going to do? Visit a craft fair or craft shop with an adult and some other Cub Scouts and see if you can get any ideas. You could try...

▷ peg models
▷ plaster casts
▷ knitting
▷ pipe cleaner art
▷ soap carving

Badge link

WHY NOT TRY
THE CRAFTSMAN
BADGE?

OVER TO YOU

You might have other ideas for things to do in this Section of your Adventure Crest Award. Speak with a Leader before you do it and then see how well you can do your chosen idea.

*Choose at least **one** activity from Creativity.*

Your Community

INTRODUCTION

This section lets you help your community in some way. At the same time, you will be able to find out a lot about where you live.

You must choose at least ONE of the five activities in this section.

1. COMMUNITY HELP
Do something to help a local hospital, place of worship, old people's or children's home or the disabled.

There are lots of ways you and your Pack can brighten up the lives of other people. Why not plan some entertainment with your friends, including singing, a short sketch or play and some mime and music. You could then go and perform it at an old people's home or hospital.

Collect books or magazines in good condition and give them to a hospital or old persons home. Collect comics or games in good condition and give them to a local children's home or to a children's charity.

2. COMMUNITY GROUPS
Take part in a local activity at a fête, gala or other event organised by a group outside Scouting.

You can find out about a local community group (eg. Rotary Clubs, Church fête, Red Cross, R.S.P.B., School, etc.) by asking an adult you know, watching the school noticeboard, looking outside local places of worship or in the local paper. There may be some exciting events coming up in the near future.

If you are going to be useful and helpful, you need a job to do. It may be a messy job like sorting jumble, or hard work, like putting out rows of chairs and tables for bazaars, serving refreshments and so on. Some community groups take old people shopping, deliver firewood or arrange outings.

Ask if you can help.

WIN A
COCONUT
AND HELP A
LOCAL
CHARITY

*Choose at least **one** activity from Your Community.*

Your Community

3. COMMUNITY PROJECT

Help plan and take part in a project to improve the surroundings in your area.

Find out if there is a local conservation project in your area and offer to help in some way. Clear footpaths, canal towpaths or parks, of weeds and rubbish. Write to the local park rangers, the Council or an environmental group for other ideas.

Instead, you might like to take part in a project to collect old newspapers for recycling, old clothes for developing countries and so on. Your Leader will help you decide what to do.

Remember to...decide how long you want the project to last,

...ask permission and ask for adult supervision if necessary,

...think of the availability and cost of any materials you may need to use.

Badge link

WHY NOT TRY THE WORLD CONSERVATION BADGE?

4. PEOPLE WHO HELP

Meet or visit someone in your area who helps the community and complete a project that will help them.

Contact one of the organisations shown below, or another of your own choice, which are in your area and ask them if they need any help in a forthcoming event and offer the services of you or your Pack. Consider what you need to do to complete the task.

Help the Aged
The Red Cross
St. John Ambulance

R.S.P.C.A.
R.N.L.I.
Local place of worship.

CHECKLIST

JOB	Stack chairs after Church coffee morning
DATE	Sunday 1st November
WHERE	St. Cuthberts
CONTACT	Mrs Smith
PHONE	632104
UNIFORM	Yes

SAVE THE CHILDREN FUND

Your Community

5. LOCAL CHARITY

Find out something about a local or national charity and think up ideas of how you can help them. Send them a copy of your ideas and suggestions.

Decide which charity you want to help. Charitable organisations are always grateful to receive ideas and support — perhaps there is a local project in which you could take part.

SPONSORED WALK

SHOE SHINE

JUMBLE SALE

WHITE ELEPHANT STALL

Badge link

WHY NOT TRY THE COMMUNITY BADGE?

*Choose at least **one** activity from Your Community.*

Countries and Cultures

INTRODUCTION

Here you will be able to find out a lot about people in other countries and how they live their lives.

You must choose at least ONE of the four activities in this section.

1. INTERNATIONAL MEETING
Help organise a Pack Meeting to show what life is like in another country.

To try and feel what it is like to live in another country, help a Leader plan a special Pack Meeting based on a country you have chosen together.

You could find out things like:

▷ what food people eat
▷ the clothes they wear
▷ National costumes
▷ learn some simple phrases in their language
▷ the national flags
▷ the weather
▷ the type of money they use

Help the Leaders run a game for the whole Pack.

Draw or paint a large flag of the country to hang in your Headquarters.

Colour in these flags correctly.

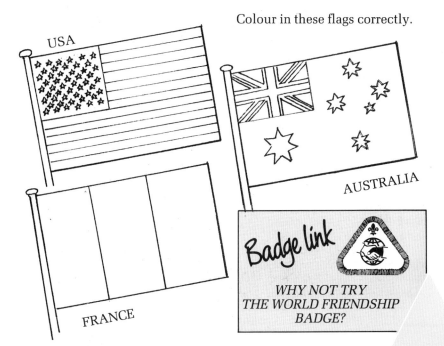

USA

AUSTRALIA

FRANCE

Badge link

WHY NOT TRY THE WORLD FRIENDSHIP BADGE?

*Choose at least **one** activity from Countries and Cultures.*

Countries and Cultures

2. INTERNATIONAL ORGANISATION

Find out about an organisation that helps people in other countries and do something to support it.

Name at least two of these organisations which you have seen on television or in the newspapers.

1 ....

2 ....

Choose any one of these international organisations and find out some more about it.

Your Leader may be able to find you the address of the organisation in the United Kingdom so you could write and ask for details. Make a poster or scrap book on what you have found out and share it with your Six.

Find out what you can do to help them. They may want old clothes, so you and your friends could arrange a small clothes collection. They may need money so perhaps you could ask your Leader if you can arrange a Pack good turn to raise money or donate some subs to the organisation.

3. INTERNATIONAL SCOUTING

Find out about Scouting in some other countries and, if possible, make contact with some Scouts from abroad.

Scouts throughout the world wear different uniforms and badges but the common link between them all is the World Membership Badge which you also wear on your uniform. All Scouts have a Promise and Law, although the words may differ from country to country.

Akela will be able to give you some information about Scouts overseas and perhaps you can find out some of the games and activities they do. You and your Pack may be able to contact some Cubs overseas by sending them a tape or letter.

What to find out:
▷ what uniform do they wear?
▷ what badges do they have?
▷ where do they meet?

▷ when do they meet?
▷ how old are they?
▷ what activities do they do?
▷ what is their Promise?

*Choose at least **one** activity from Countries and Cultures.*

Countries and Cultures

4. OTHER PEOPLES' CULTURES

Find out something about the traditions, customs and religions of a culture other than your own.

The world is a large place but it is important that we all live in peace together. To do this we need to know something about the people around us who may have different traditions and cultures.

Your style of life may be different from your friends' or other Cub Scouts'.

Some things to do...

▷ find out about a form of worship different from your own

▷ visit a place of worship different from your own

▷ have a taste evening, where you can sample some foods from other lands.

CHRISTIANITY

JUDAISM

HINDUISM

BUDDHISM

ISLAM

SIKH

Badge link

WHY NOT TRY
THE WORLD FAITHS
BADGE?

*Choose at least **one** activity from Countries and Cultures.*

My Promise

INTRODUCTION

How well are you keeping your Cub Scout Promise? Can you still remember it? You should think about it every day as it will help you to be a better person as you grow up.

You must complete BOTH parts of this section.

1. *Make up a prayer about a Pack Activity or meeting in which you are taking part and share it with others.*

You probably say a prayer at your Pack Meeting. Your Leader may let you think up a prayer for one evening or read a prayer at the end of a special activity.

2. *When you have completed most of the activities for this award, talk to a Leader about them and how you have tried to put your Promise and Law into practice in everything you have done.*

When you were invested you promised to do your duty to God and to the Queen, to help other people and to

	How have I shown that I was keeping my Promise?	How am I going to try to keep my Promise?	How well have I done? Good/fair? (tick box)
Duty to God			
Duty to the Queen			
Helping other people			

keep the Cub Scout Law. The Cub Scout Law says that you think of others before yourself and do a good turn every day.

Fill in the boxes above to show how you have kept your Promise. In the second group of boxes make a few plans to keep your Promise during the next few weeks and then look back to see how well you have done.

Now talk to your Leader about this.

Badge link

WHY NOT TRY THE MY FAITH BADGE?

*Complete **both** activities from My Promise.*

Scout Family Badge

INTRODUCTION

As soon as you complete these TWO Activities you will receive a Scout Family Badge to wear on your uniform

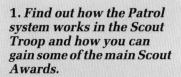

▷ Find out the names of the Patrols in your local Scout Troop.
▷ What are the names of the main Scout Awards?
▷ Find out some of the activities you have to do to gain the first of the Scout Awards.
▷ What does the Patrol Leaders' Council do?

2. *Take part in an activity with some Scouts.*

LOOKING AHEAD

This is a chance for you to see for yourself what Scouts do and join in the fun.

Akela may be able to arrange for you and some of your friends to meet Scouts from your local Troop.

Now you are getting older you can look forward to working on the Scout Membership Award as you move from Cub Scouts into Scouts. Have a great time!

1. *Find out how the Patrol system works in the Scout Troop and how you can gain some of the main Scout Awards.*

PATROL SYSTEM

Scouts are boys and girls aged between about 10½ and 15½ years old. Each Scout Troop is made up of Patrols — which are a bit like Sixes — usually named after animals or birds. The Patrol is led by a Patrol Leader who helps run the Troop as a member of the Patrol Leaders' Council.

ADVENTURE CREST AWARD

THIS IS TO CERTIFY

NAME ....

OF THE ....

has completed the Adventure Crest Award.

.... AKELA

SIGNED ....

DATE ....

*Complete **both** activities from the Scout Family Badge.*

The Cub Scout Challenge

INTRODUCTION

By the time you are 9½ years old, you will already have tried some activities with your Pack, now here are some more for you to enjoy. The Cub Scout Challenge is an extra award which you might like to try to gain.

Make sure that you choose activities that you haven't already done for one of the other awards. By talking to a Leader you should be able to decide on some new challenges which will give you a chance to try new and more exciting things.

You may want to do some of the activities in the Cub Scout Challenge with the rest of the Pack or with your Six. You must show that you have taken a large and active part in them and even organised or helped to organise some of them. For example, you might lead a team or help younger Cub Scouts with parts of an activity which they find difficult.

CHECKLIST

DATE COMPLETED

▷ Outdoor Challenge

▷ Adventure Challenge

▷ Sharing Together

▷ Helping to Lead

You must complete activities in EACH of the FOUR sections of the Cub Scout Challenge.

Outdoor Challenge

Outdoor activities are always exciting and this challenge includes a number of outdoor projects. You will need to talk to a Leader about the best way in which to tackle this challenge.

It may be that you will complete all of this section while you are at camp or on a long outing, or you may do them at different times. Whenever you take part in these activities remember that you are being asked to do something a little more exciting and difficult than you would expect the younger Cub Scouts in your Pack to do.

Take part in an 'outdoor challenge' with a Leader and other Cub Scouts which should include at least FOUR of the following activities:

1. *Spend at least two nights under canvas;*

Where will you choose to go? You may be able to go on a Cub Camp. There will be things to find out such as how to look after your tent and to keep warm at night. Some things will be different, you can't take your bed with you, so what are you going to use? How will you keep everything tidy inside your tent? One thing is for sure. It will be an adventure to remember.

Badge link

WHY NOT TRY THE CAMPER BADGE?

*Choose **four** activities in Outdoor Challenge.*

Outdoor Challenge

2. Plan and go on a hike;

When you go on a hike you need to make sure that you take everything that you will need and that you have planned the route carefully. One of the most important things is to wear comfortable shoes!

3. Cook a simple meal, 'backwoods' style;

To do this you will need to light a fire out-of-doors. Decide what you would like to cook and then find out how you would cook it without a cooker or microwave oven. This is 'backwoods' style cooking which means you don't use any usual kitchen utensils like frying pans, and cookers. You can use aluminium foil. You will need to be very careful because fire can be a dangerous enemy as well as a useful friend, so watch out!

Make sure that you do not plan to walk too far. About six kilometres will be a good distance to aim for.

Badge link

WHY NOT TRY THE CAMPER BADGE?

Badge link

WHY NOT TRY THE EXPLORER BADGE?

*Choose **four** activities in Outdoor Challenge.*

Outdoor Challenge

4. Take part in a wide game;

Your wide game could take place anywhere — in a field, a park or in the woods. It may have a story attached to it.

You will have to listen carefully to the rules as the game may take longer than usual and you will have to remember them for the whole game. You may need to help some of the younger Cub Scouts who are a little less sure of themselves.

5. Build a Bivouac;

Think what you would do if you were stranded and needed a shelter to keep you safe, warm

and dry. What sort of natural materials would you need? Would it depend on where you were? If you were out in the open what would you use without damaging the living things around you or their homes?

6. Follow a simple orienteering course;

Do you like treasure hunts with clues and hidden treasure?

My first is in green, My second in blue. Three strides West —— Here's what to do...

If so, then you will enjoy this activity. You may have to race against time to visit all the bases before arriving at the finishing line. There will be clues to follow which are written as compass directions or lots of puzzles to solve.

7. Or any other suitable activity agreed with your Leader.

Badge link

WHY NOT TRY THE NAVIGATOR BADGE?

*Choose **four** activities in Outdoor Challenge.*

Adventure Challenge

With a Leader choose and take part in at least TWO adventurous activities.

All adventurous activities have some rules about safety which you must obey to avoid getting hurt.

Here are some challenges you might be able to take part in:

▷ night hike
▷ assault course
▷ a camp with other older Cub Scouts
▷ simple canoeing
▷ sailing
▷ rafting
▷ basic rock climbing
▷ climbing wall
▷ pioneering project
▷ abseiling

Choose an adventurous activity and write down some rules which you would need to obey whilst doing it:

1 ....
....
2 ....
....
3 ....
....
4 ....
....
5 ....
....

Talk to your Leaders about these safety rules.

*Choose **two** activities from Adventure Challenge.*

Sharing Together

Take part in at least three meetings of older Cub Scouts and Leaders, share ideas for future Pack meetings, events and outings and help make some plans for one of them.

Your Pack may have a Sixers' meeting. This is where the Sixers meet with Akela for a short while, maybe before, during or after a Pack meeting, to talk about what they would like to do in the future.

Look through the following lists and choose some ideas and add some of your own.

Some ideas for Pack meetings:
1. A quiz evening
2. A games evening
3. An explorer evening
4. ....
5. ....
6. ....

Some ideas for events:
1. Running a stall at a fête
2. Older Cub Scouts' camp
3. A Pack open night
4. ....
5. ....
6. ....

Some ideas for outings:
1. Swimming
2. A visit to an old building
3. The zoo or nature park
4. A museum
5. ....
6. ....
7. ....

*Take part in **three** meetings from Sharing Together.*

Helping to Lead

Take a LEADING PART in two Pack activities, such as —

▷ TEAM CAPTAIN

Act as a captain for a football, swimming or cricket team or another team of your choice.

It is not always easy being a leader. You will need to remember that some of your Six or team will be younger than you or new to the Pack so you will have to explain things carefully and check that they understand what you want them to do.

Remember that it is up to you to welcome other teams if they are visiting you or thank a team if you are playing away. Perhaps you could make sure that whether you win or lose, you always give the other team three cheers and thank them for the game. Don't forget to say thank you to the officials, umpires, linesmen and other helpers and especially whoever has to wash the team's kit!

Badge link

WHY NOT TRY THE SPORTSMAN BADGE?

▷ DISTRICT/COUNTY/ AREA EVENT

Represent your Pack at a District or County/Area event such as a competition, quiz, Sixers' Meeting or any other suitable event.

This is an exciting opportunity for you to show other people what your Pack is like, and meet other Cub Scouts.

Make sure that you congratulate your team — whether they win or lose. Remind them that they should be having fun by taking part just as much as trying to win.

DISTRICT QUIZ

QUESTIONS

BLUE SIX

*Choose **two** activities from Helping to Lead.*

Helping to Lead

▷ CAMPING
Be a tent leader or take on a special responsibility at camp.

Before you go to camp, talk to a Leader about the sort of jobs which will need doing. It may be helping with the cooking or laying the table, or helping to look after one of the younger Cub Scouts who has never been away from home before.

If you are a tent leader, try not to be too bossy but help everyone who goes to camp to have a good time.

▷ PACK SHOW
Take a leading role in a Pack Show either front or back stage.

Some people like to be on the stage and others prefer to help where they can't be seen.

Which do you like?

Badge link

WHY NOT TRY
THE CAMPER
BADGE?

Badge link

WHY NOT TRY
THE ENTERTAINER
BADGE?

THE CUB SCOUT CHALLENGE

*Choose **two** activities from Helping to Lead.*

Helping to Lead

▷ PACK OPEN NIGHT
Help with the arrangements for a Pack Open Night.

Here is a list of some ideas of how you could help. Can you add to it?

	TICK WHEN DONE
▷ send out invitations	
▷ make posters	
▷ make cakes	
▷ welcome visitors at the door	
▷ organise the clearing up	
▷ wash up after the refreshments	
▷ make a slide/tape presentation to be shown during the evening	
▷	
▷	
▷	

▷ BEAVER SCOUT COLONY
Visit a Colony to tell Beaver Scouts about Cub Scouts and help run a game at a Colony meeting.

You will need to talk to both your Leader and the Beaver Scout Leader to help you to decide on a suitable game.

Remember the Beaver Scouts are much younger than you and will need very simple rules and instructions. When you talk to them about Cub Scouts, remember to tell them about the fun and adventures that they will have.

You will find it easier to talk if you have some pictures or a poster, or some slides to show.

94

*Choose **two** activities from Helping to Lead.*

Helping to Lead

▷ ACT OF WORSHIP
Help plan and take part in an Act of Worship.

Your act of worship could be at camp, during a Pack Meeting, at a church parade or any other suitable occasion at your place of worship and should include some happy songs and some prayers.

If there is someone you would like to come to join your Act of Worship, you will need to send them a proper invitation to say exactly what you would like them to do and for how long.

Do you have a Pack prayer book? If so, you could add part of your Act of Worship to it.

Badge link

WHY NOT TRY THE MY FAITH BADGE?

▷ CONSERVATION
Help other Cub Scouts carry out a Local Conservation project.

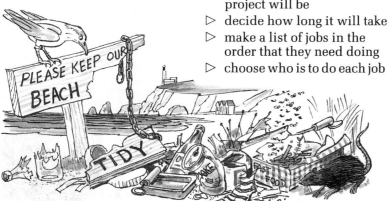

PLEASE KEEP OUR BEACH

TIDY

Here is a checklist to help you to plan and prepare a project which would help improve your local surroundings:
▷ what needs doing?
▷ decide on how big the project will be
▷ decide how long it will take
▷ make a list of jobs in the order that they need doing
▷ choose who is to do each job
▷ decide how you will tell people what you have done
▷ write to the local newspaper

For some of these things you will want help from a Leader or another grown up. By talking it through with them you can draw up your own list to help you work through the project.

Badge link

WHY NOT TRY THE WORLD CONSERVATION BADGE?

*Choose **two** activities from Helping to Lead.*

Helping to Lead

▷ **GAMES**

Organise and help run some games on a Pack night.

By watching your Leaders you can begin to learn how games are run at Meetings and you can use some of their ideas when it is your turn.

It would be nice to introduce a new game, but you should always start with a game that everyone knows and likes. Explain the rules clearly and make sure that you understand what everyone is meant to be doing.

▷ **OVER TO YOU**

Take a leading part in any other suitable activity decided between you and a Leader.

You and your Leader probably have some good ideas which you would like to try out.

You could start a Pack ideas book, or take your idea to a Sixers' meeting or swap it with a Cub Scout from another Pack. You could also write to the Cub Scout Supplement of:

SCOUTING Magazine at Baden-Powell House, Queens Gate, LONDON SW7 5JS.

Don't waste a good idea – share it!!

CUB SCOUT CHALLENGE

THIS IS TO CERTIFY

NAME ....

OF THE ....

has completed the Cub Scout Challenge.

SIGNED .... AKELA

DATE ....

CUB SCOUT *Challenge*

*Choose **two** activities from Helping to Lead.*

My Personal Record

 SCOUT MEMBERSHIP BADGE

. . . .

 ADVENTURE CREST AWARD

. . . .

 SCOUT FAMILY BADGE

. . . .

CUB SCOUT CHALLENGE

. . . .

 SCOUT FAMILY BADGE

. . . .

 ADVENTURE AWARD

. . . .

 SCOUT FAMILY BADGE

. . . .

 THE CUB SCOUT AWARD

. . . .

 SCOUT FAMILY BADGE

. . . .

 CUB SCOUT MEMBERSHIP AWARD

. . . .

JOINED THE PACK ON

. . . .

 **MADE A SECOND** . . . .

 **MADE A SIXER** . . . .

97

INTRODUCTION

While you are working on your main Awards, you will also have the chance to try some Activity Badges.

▷ Some badges you might work for at Pack meetings
▷ Some badges you might be able to prepare for at home
▷ Some badges you might earn on outings and at camps
▷ Some badges are earned in three stages
▷ Some badges you might do on your own and others you might work for in small groups.

For every badge you will have had to work hard and to a high standard, so you can wear your badge with pride. You can start working on these badges as soon as you join the Pack.

The badges cover a wide range of hobbies, skills and interests.

Choose the ones you are interested in, perhaps from something you have liked in your main Awards.

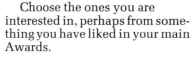

GARDENER

ARTIST

ENTERTAINER

COLLECTOR

EXPLORER

HANDYMAN

COOK

CAMPER

ATHLETE

WRITER

COLLECTING?

SPORT?

SCIENCE?

98

Animal Lover

Choose any THREE of the following alternatives.

1. Visit a zoo or wildlife park and find out about some of the feeding habits and natural habitats of some of the animals and creatures you see.
2. Take care of a pet. Know the correct foods to give it and how to recognise and prevent common illnesses and how to treat them.
3. Help to care for a farm animal, know the correct food to give it and how to look after it. Know how to recognise the common illnesses and what special care is needed before and after the birth of farm animals.
4. Keep a record over two weeks, in pictures, sketches, photographs or tape recordings, of bird, animal or insect life in your garden or local area/park.
5. Know six different freshwater, seawater or tropical fish and know what types of foods they eat.
6. Belong to an animal, bird or wildlife society. Either take part in one of its activities or make progress in any award scheme offered.
7. Make a poster, collage or drawing about the dangers in the countryside that threaten wildlife and talk to the examiner about it.

Artist

1. Know the primary colours and demonstrate how to mix paints to make other colours.
2. Choose three other activities from the list below. One of these activities is to be done in the presence of the examiner:

a) Draw with pencil, brush, pen or crayon an original illustration of any imaginary incident, character or scene.
b) Design and make a greetings card.
c) Make a poster advertising Cub Scouting or a Cub Scout event.
d) Make a design and print it on paper or fabric, e.g. using potato or lino cuts.
e) Design and make a decorated book cover.
f) Draw or paint a picture from observation.
g) Complete any other suitable activity agreed with the examiner.

Astronomer

1. Make a model or draw a diagram of the Solar System.
2. Explain the difference between a star and a planet.
3. Identify and find the Pole Star and at least three other constellations.

4. Find out and present some information about two of the following:-
   Comets
   Northern Lights
   Eclipses
   Meteorites
   Sun spots
   Black holes
   Asteroids
   Light years
   Space exploration

5. Observe the moon, if possible using binoculars or telescope, and describe some of its features.

(Note: Never look at the sun with binoculars or telescope as it will damage your eyes.)

Athlete

A THREE STAGE BADGE
(Badges for successive stages may be worn at the same time).

You must gain the following points: 5 points for Stage 1; 8 points for Stage 2 and 10 points for Stage 3. You should add up the scores from your **best** four events.

Sargent Jump

	3 points	2 points	1 point
1. 50 metres Sprint	9 secs	10 secs	11 secs
2. Throwing the Cricket Ball — using 135g (4¾ oz) ball			
	25 metres (82′)	22 metres (72′)	18 metres (60′)
3. High Jump	96 cms (3′2″)	86 cms (2′10″)	76 cms (2′6″)
4. Long Jump	3 metres (10′)	2.5 metres (8′)	2 metres (6′6″)
5. Sargent Jump — measurements refer to height on target			
	35 cm (14″)	30 cm (12″)	25 cm (10″)
6. Shuttle Run — individual runs 6 × 10 metres			
	18 secs	19 secs	20 secs
7. 50 metres Skipping — with rope turning overhead			
	12 secs	13 secs	14 secs
8. 1,000 metres Run	5 mins	6 mins	10 mins

Note:
When requirement 3 is undertaken, special regard must be given to the nature of the jump, and the landing facilities required. Unless expert tuition and supervision is available, the Fosbury Flop must not be attempted.

When requirement 6 is undertaken, the limits of the run are marked on the ground, and the runner's hand or foot must touch on, or above, the mark at the end of the run.

Book Reader

1. Produce a list of at least 6 books you have read or used recently, name their authors and be able to tell the examiner something about three of the books. The three books to be chosen by you are to include at least one story and at least one factual book.

Note: The three books must be of a reasonable standard, taking the Cub Scout's age and development into account.

2. Show that you understand how to care for books.

3. Show that you can use a dictionary, encyclopaedia and an atlas.

4. Explain to the examiner how the books in a library are set out and how to find fiction and non-fiction books.

Camper

1. With other Cub Scouts, camp under canvas for at least three nights (not necessarily on the same occasion).

2. Help pack your kit for a Cub Scout camp.

3. Help pitch and strike a tent and know how to care for it.

4. At camp, help to prepare, cook, serve and clear away a meal, if possible out of doors.

5. Know the basic health and safety rules for camp and how to prepare for tent and kit inspection.

6. Take part in at least one of the following activities while at camp:
   a) Camp fire
   b) Scout's Own
   c) Wide Game
   d) Joint activity with other Cub Scouts on site or from a local Group
   e) A Good Turn for the site
   f) Any suitable similar activity.
   g) Help to tidy up the camp site before you leave.

Collector

1. Make a collection over a period of three months of a number of similar items (e.g. stamps, postcards, matchboxes or fossils).
2. Arrange your collection neatly and in a suitable order, labelling items correctly and clearly.
3. Talk about items in your collection that particularly interest you.
4. Visit or look at a collection made by someone else and explain what you like or dislike about the presentation of the collection, choice of venue, etc. This could be a personal or public collection.

Note: A Cub Scout may gain and wear any number of Collector Badges.

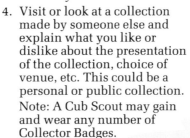

Communicator

1. Demonstrate how to use a private and public telephone and if possible use a phone card.
2. Know how to make an emergency telephone call.
3. Choose any three of the following activities:
   a) Find out about and make use of at least two of the following:
      facsimile machine (FAX), answering machine, walkie talkie, teletext, cellular phone, electronic mail, Citizen Band (C.B.) radio, or any other communication system.
   b) Make a verbal or taped report of a local event either past or present.
   c) Write and decipher three simple messages using codes, ciphers or invisible ink.
   d) Hold a simple conversation in another language.
   e) Make and maintain a link over a short time with another Cub Scout Pack using tapes, videos, letters, etc.
   f) Find out how other people with a visual or hearing impairment communicate, e.g. Braille, sign language, etc.
   f) Memorise a message and deliver it 20 minutes later.
   g) Pass a message to someone else using Amateur Radio.

Community

1. Visit a local emergency service station such as the Police, fire, ambulance services, Coast Guard or Mountain Rescue. Find out how the Station is run and organised.
2. Know what information you should give to the emergency services over the telephone and make sure you know how to make an emergency phone call.

3. Know some precautions you can take to protect home and possessions against crime.
4. Mark on a map or chart the services and organisations that help your Community such as, doctor, age concern, fire or police station, meals on wheels, etc.
5. Draw a picture or write a slogan which will encourage children to respect the property of other people and discourage vandalism.
6. Know the importance of marking property so that it can be returned to the owner if it has been recovered after being stolen. Know about ultra-violet pens and the use of names and addresses and post codes. Know the importance of keeping numbers of bicycles, etc.

Computer

1. Know the various parts of a computer system and demonstrate what each is used for, e.g. disc drive or cassette, keyboard, screen, printer, joystick, mouse.
2. Show a basic knowledge of a computer keyboard and its functions.
3. Find a particular program from magnetic storage and load it into the computer.

4. Write and save a short program to perform **one** of the following operations:
   a) To print out multiplication tables.
   b) To calculate on which day of the week you were born.
   c) To add together numbers which you input from the keyboard.
   d) To make the computer prompt responses to questions.
   e) To make the computer respond 'Good morning' or 'Good afternoon' as appropriate.
5. Describe at least five uses to which a computer can be put in everyday life.

6. Make a list of programs you have used recently and be prepared to talk about them with the examiner.
7. Explain at least one of the following types of software: data base, spreadsheet, word processing.

Cook

1. Discuss with the examiner the advantages and disadvantages of different methods of preparing and cooking food and the importance of a balanced diet.
2. Plan, cook, serve and clear away a two course meal for at least two people.

   The following dishes are given as suggestions. You may produce your own menu which will be approved by the examiner beforehand.

   Main Courses

   A mince dish, such as shepherds pie, spaghetti bolognaise, curry.
   A salad dish, e.g. cheese, egg or meat.
   A fish dish, e.g. fish pie, kippers, etc.
   A vegetarian dish, e.g. vegetable lasagne, nut roast, etc.

   Sweets

   Baked apple with custard
   Fruit crumble
   Fresh fruit salad
   Trifle
   Banana split

3. Prepare and cook fresh vegetables.
4. Make either scones, small cakes, biscuits or tarts.
5. Make and serve a hot drink.
6. Know the basic rules of safety and hygiene in the kitchen and the reasons for them.

Craftsman

You must complete three activities to a high standard, one of which must be completed in the presence of the examiner.

1. Make a model out of clay and fire it in a kiln if appropriate.
2. Make a decorative article from cane, raffia, wool, leather, wood or any other suitable material approved in advance by the examiner.
3. Design a print on fabric or paper, e.g. screen printing, fabric print, lino print, etc.
4. Make a toy, puppet or model of your own design.
5. Make a collage using a variety of materials, e.g. natural materials, cloth, felt, wool.
6. Find a natural object such as a piece of wood or a stone that has an interesting shape. Clean, rub down and varnish it, then mount it to make an ornament.
7. Undertake a project, having agreed it with the examiner, involving the use of a plastic or metal construction kit such as Meccano. The standard expected should demand an imaginative approach and a high quality of workmanship.
8. Complete a project in a craft technique, such as marbling, origami, string work, macrame, papier mache, plaster casts, weaving or other craft agreed with the examiner.

Cyclist

1. Own or have the regular use of a bicycle of suitable size.
2. Be able to mount and dismount properly.
3. Understand the need for keeping the bicycle in a roadworthy condition, and help to do this.
4. Be able to clean and oil a bicycle. Show how to pump up the tyres and how to mend a puncture.
5. Understand the need for keeping a bicycle locked when leaving it unattended.
6. Show a knowledge of the proper use of those signals and rules applicable to cyclists as set out in the Highway Code in the Section for the Road User on Wheels and Extra Rules for Cyclists.
7. Understand the need for lights and reflective clothing. Talk about the safety measures necessary for riding in poor light.
8. Under observation go for a short ride in a safe place to show that you can ride safely and confidently.

Entertainer

Carry out at least two of the following either with a group of other Cub Scouts or by yourself.

1. Help to make up a mime or play and perform it.
2. Perform a puppet play or shadowgraph using puppets which you have made.
3. Help to plan and make an entertainment recorded on video or audio tape.
4. Sing a programme of songs, carols or hymns.
5. Perform some folk or traditional dances.
6. Make a selection of rhythm instruments and use as accompaniments.
7. Take part in a gymnastic display.
8. Make up and perform a dance to a piece of music of your own choice.
9. Help plan and perform a series of magic tricks.
10 Take part in a gang show, concert or band performance.
11. Or any other suitable activity agreed with the examiner.

Explorer

1. Know the preparation required for a one day expedition in the countryside, e.g. cost, correct clothing, footwear, first-aid kit and food.
2. Take part in two Cub Scout expeditions out of doors, one of which should include a hike of at least 5 kilometres (3 miles).
3. Build and light a fire outdoors and use it to make a hot drink.

4. Build a simple shelter.
5. Find your way along a route of at least 1 kilometre (half a mile) using one of the following methods:
   * compass
   * maps
   * landmarks
   * tracking signs
   * clues
   * codes.

First Aider

1. Know your limits of first aid and when you would get adult help.
2. Know how to control bleeding by direct pressure on a wound.
3. Know the importance of cleanliness and show how to dress minor cuts and grazes with gauze and a roller bandage; apply and remove adhesive dressings.

4. Demonstrate the use of a triangular bandage as an arm sling, knee and head bandage.
5. Know how to treat burns and scalds and how to put out burning clothing.
6. Know how to treat a wasp and bee sting and how to remove a splinter.
7. Have a knowledge of mouth-to-mouth resuscitation and where possible, demonstrate this method by use of a manakin or other appropriate aid.
8. Demonstrate how to make a patient comfortable.

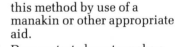

Gardener

1. Either:
   a) Look after a patch of garden, know what tools are needed and how to use and look after them. Grow something in your garden suitable for the time of year.

   Or: b) Grow a variety of plants indoors and know the conditions under which they must be kept.

2. Choose any two of the following:
   a) Grow vegetables or flowers from seed; know how to prick out and transplant.
   b) Know about hazards to plants and flowers (e.g. diseases, pests) and understand what preventative methods can be taken and what can be done to aid growth.
   c) Know how to store vegetables and how long they may be stored.
   d) Show how to prepare flowers for display.
   e) Make a compost heap.

   f) Carry out a soil test using a standard kit.
   g) Help plan and plant a rockery garden, a fern or herb garden, herbacious border, hanging basket, garden tub, etc.
   h) Help maintain a lawn and understand why it needs constant attention.

Handyman

1. Demonstrate the safe use of, and how to take care of, tools such as hammer, saw, screwdriver, spanner, pliers, hand drill, glue gun.
2. Demonstrate how to prepare and paint a vertical surface with paint-brushes, roller or pad and show how to clean them.

3. Complete two projects from the following list:
   Help design and make:
   ▷ a nesting box or window box
   ▷ a box for storing tools, pencils, tapes, etc.
   ▷ a rack for keys, mugs or coats
   ▷ book ends or bookstand
   ▷ a shoe rack
   ▷ notice board for camp
   ▷ letter holder
   ▷ towel rail

   ▷ any other project agreed between you and the examiner.

Health & Fitness

1. Visit or meet ONE of the following and find out how they help people to stay fit and healthy:

   Doctor, Dentist, Optician, Chemist, Chiropodist, Osteopath, Health Visitor, District Nurse or any other suitable person. Make a poster about good health and ask if it can be displayed in their waiting room or office.

2. Discuss with the examiner how some of the following can damage your health: lack of exercise, smoking, drinking, solvent abuse.

3. Record all the things you have done in a week which have contributed to your personal hygiene and cleanliness.

4. Either:

   (a) Visit one of the facilities in your area which promotes health and fitness (e.g. Leisure Centre, swimming pool, sports club etc.) and find out what health and fitness facilities they have and make use of one of them.

   Or:

   (b) Keep a diary of all the physical activities which help you stay fit and healthy.

5. Prepare and serve one meal from a menu for two people and explain how preparation and cooking methods contribute to healthy eating.

6. Show you know how and why food is labelled and stored in shops and at home.

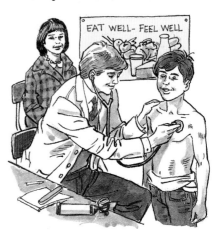

Hobbies

1. Show a continuing interest in your chosen hobby for at least three months.

2. Demonstrate to the examiner how you pursue your hobby and what equipment, materials and background information you have used.

3. Discuss with the examiner how you plan to develop your hobby or skill in the future.

Note: You may gain and wear any number of Hobbies Badges.

Home Help

1. Under adult supervision cook a simple one course meal.
2. Lay a table correctly and serve a simple meal. (This can be done in conjunction with 1 above).
3. Wash up afterwards and show how to deal with a saucepan or similar cooking utensils, cutlery, glassware, etc.

4. Under adult supervision, wash and iron your Group scarf.
5. Sew on a badge or button.
6. Keep your room clean and tidy and make your bed for a week.
7. Clean two of the following:- windows, silver, brasswork, basin/bath, cupboard.
8. Clean and tidy a living room.

Home Safety

1. Know what to do in the event of a burst water pipe, gas leak or electricity power failure in your home.
2. Know what precautions you need to take and what to do if fire breaks out in your home.
3. Be able to identify the common causes of accidents in the home and how they can be prevented.

4. Know what should be checked to protect your home from a burglary if you are going away on holiday.

5. Know how to make an emergency telephone call to all the emergency services and know where the nearest public telephone box is to your house, or where you can make an emergency call should your phone be out of action.

6. Make a list of useful emergency telephone numbers and addresses and display them in your home: i.e. the Doctor, Dentist, Vet, Police Station, relatives.

Local Historian

Choose any three of the following alternatives.

1. Find out about someone who lived in or near your town who was famous, or visit and find out about a famous old building, monument, earthwork or other place of historical interest. Make a log book or scrap book and discuss what you have found out with the examiner.

2. Find out the meaning of, and collect pictures of either your County, Borough, District, Town or Village coat of arms. Tell the examiner how many different places you have seen the coat of arms displayed.

3. Talk to someone who has lived in your area for a long time and find out about what they did at your age, and what changes they have seen in your area over the past years.

4. Choose two different locations in your area such as a road, park, field, hill, lake, stream and find out how they got their names.

5. Draw a map of your area and mark on it places of historical interest for visitors.

6. With your examiner, go on a short walk of your choice in your area and describe to him local points of historical interest.

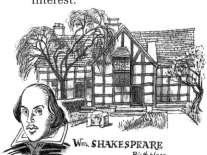

Wm. SHAKESPEARE
Birthplace

Map Reader

1. Understand the principal signs and symbols used on a 1:50,000 scale Ordnance Survey map of your locality. Be able to pin-point your home and Scout Headquarters. Explain how well known local features of your choice are represented on the map.

2. Make a scale model of an 80 metre (250 ft) hill — showing the contour layers at regular intervals.

3. Describe what you would see along a 5 kilometre (3 miles) stretch of road set by the examiner on any 1:50,000 Ordnance Survey map.

4. Show you can use 6 figure grid references.

5. Know how to use a compass and set a map.

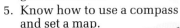

Musician

1. Explain the major symbols on a musical score and give the correct meaning of common musical terms.
2. Sing two songs or play two pieces of your own choice which show different styles and tempos.
3. Choose any two of the following alternatives:
   (a) Sight read a simple piece of music set by the examiner.
   (b) Demonstrate some musical exercises which improve your playing or singing.
   (c) Name the parts of your musical instrument or know how your voice works.
   (d) Know how to look after your musical instrument or voice.
   (e) Clap out the rhythm of three pieces played by the examiner.
   (f) Listen to a piece of music and name some of the musical instruments heard.
   (g) Know the storyline of an opera, ballet or folk song.

My Faith

1. Collect together, over a period of three months, all you can about being a member of your religious faith. The collection can be a scrap book, it may include pictures, photographs, tapes, etc. The collection will be of anything to do with the life at your place of worship.

   Before you start making your Collection, talk about it with a Leader, someone at home and at your place of worship.

You might include:
▷ Pictures of important objects at your place of worship
▷ tape-recordings of favourite religious songs
▷ names of people and what they do at your place of worship
▷ special festivals
▷ stories you have heard or read from your religious book(s)
▷ some of your favourite prayers
▷ a record of any special activity that you take part in, at your place of worship
▷ ways in which you have helped others.
And there are many other things you may want to include.

2. When you have finished your collection show it to your Minister, Priest or Church Leader. Tell them about all you have done for this badge.

The badge is awarded by the Cub Scout Leader in consultation with the Minister, Priest or Church Leader.

Naturalist

Do any THREE of the following:

1. Make a survey of a hedgerow or wild area and be able to identify at least six species of wild flowers, grasses or ferns.
2. Keep a record of birds you have spotted over one week and be able to identify at least six wild birds.
3. Make a survey of a pond, river, stream or seashore and be able to identify some animal, insect or plant life you find.
4. Explore the insect life of a particular area and be able to identify some of the types of insects you find.
5. Identify six different trees or shrubs from their leaves, shape, fruit or nuts and make a bark rubbing.
6. Identify six butterflies and or moths and talk to the examiner about their life cycle.

Navigator

1. Go for a walk or car journey with an adult around your local area, using one or more of the following methods of navigation:-
    (a) written directions
    (b) taped instructions
    (c) road signs
    (d) tracking signs
2. Find a number of routes between two given places and choose the most practical and safe for a blind or physically handicapped person. Explain your choice and tell the examiner what could be done to make the route safer.
3. By drawing a map, direct someone from your meeting place to a local railway or bus station, hospital, doctor, Post Office, etc.
4. Using a local street map, find certain roads and places of interest as requested by the examiner.
5. Help plan, or take part in, a treasure hunt using clues, directions and signs to reach a secret destination.

Personal Safety

1. Show that you know the dangers of playing on or near two of the following:- railways, busy roads, building sites, canal banks, sand/gravel pits, farm yards, river banks, quarries.
2. Take part in a fire drill and know what precautions to take to protect your home, Scout Headquarters, Pack Camp or Pack Holiday, against the risk of fire.
3. Show you can use at least one of the following codes:- Green Cross Code, Water Safety Code, Bathing Code, Firework Code etc., and make up a safety code of your own choice:- e.g. car passenger, train passenger, playground.
4. Know how to use a public telephone and how to make an emergency phone call.
5. Tell the examiner what you must do if a stranger starts to talk to you and what you must tell your parents/guardians about, if you are going out without them.
6. Know some of the hazards you may find when you are in at least one of the following:- seaside, large town, countryside, mountainous area, lakeland or moorland.

Photographer

1. Understand the features of the camera you are using and show that you know about lens focusing and apertures and their use in taking good pictures.
2. Be able to identify good practice and common mistakes in taking pictures.
3. Understand the different types of film available for different types of camera, video or cine camera.
4. Use the above skills and take a set of 12 pictures, or a short movie or video film on a theme of your choice.
5. Present a display of photographs or give a film/video show.

Scientist

Choose three experiments from each section (six in total) of the badge and explain to and/or show the examiner what you have done. Where appropriate explain any conclusions you have made.

The Physical World

1. Make a simple switch from household items and demonstrate how it could be used to control a light bulb and battery.

2. Demonstrate that electrical currents produce magnetic, chemical and heating effects and explain what happens.
3. Show that hot air rises.
4. Make an artificial rainbow by splitting up a beam of white light.
5. Make a pin-hole camera and understand principles of operation, e.g. size of hole.
6. Keep simple weather records over a month (e.g. rainfall, temperature, cloud cover, wind direction).

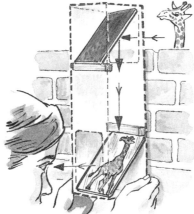

7. Make a simple compass and show the effects of metallic and magnetic materials upon it.
8. Make a simple periscope.
9. Demonstrate how to recover dissolved substances from sea water or river water.

The Living World

1. Make some yoghurt and find out how living creatures are involved in the process.
2. Grow cress (or a similar plant) and investigate what happens when light and water are excluded from it.
3. Use a net and jar to find out how many different creatures live in the water and mud at the edge of a pond.
4. Set up a wormery or ant colony and record activity over a few weeks.
5. Grow a bean or pea. When the root and shoot are visible investigate what happens when the seed is turned upside down and left to continue growing.

6. Collect seeds from various plants and discover how these are protected and dispersed.
7. Grow or make crystals or make crystal shapes from paper.
8. Investigate what happens to your pulse rate before and after exercise.

Note: Other experiments of comparable standard are acceptable if agreed with the examiner beforehand.

Sportsman

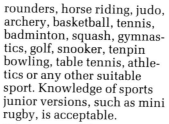

1. Show a good sportsmanlike attitude in all games and sports in which you take part.
2. Be able to tell the examiner the aims and rules of two sports whether individual or team, indoor or outdoor, e.g. rugby football, association football, cricket, hockey, rounders, horse riding, judo, archery, basketball, tennis, badminton, squash, gymnastics, golf, snooker, tenpin bowling, table tennis, athletics or any other suitable sport. Knowledge of sports junior versions, such as mini rugby, is acceptable.
3. Show reasonable proficiency and be taking an active part regularly in at least one of the above sports.
4. Show that you know the equipment and clothing necessary for the sport selected in part 2 and how to look after it, and good habits and hygiene.
5. Tell the examiner what training and preparation you take part in for your chosen sport and how and when you practise.

Swimmer

A THREE STAGE BADGE
(Badges for successive stages may
be worn at the same time).

Stage 1

Perform the following:

1. A jump or dive from the side
   of the swimming pool.
2. Breathing exercise.
3. Front glide
4. Back glide
5. Front paddle 10 metres.
6. Back paddle 10 metres.
7. Backstroke, without the use of
   arms, hands on hips, 10
   metres.
8. 25 metres of either breast-
   stroke, front crawl or back
   crawl.
9. Know the water safety rules
   and where it is safe to swim
   locally.

Stage 2

Where possible, requirements
1 to 4 to be performed in shirt and
shorts or pyjamas.

Perform the following:

1. Tread water for 1 minute in a
   vertical position.
2. A surface dive to touch the
   bottom with both hands in at
   least shoulder depth water.
3. Mushroom float for 5 seconds.
4. Swim across the width of the
   bath on any front stroke. At
   halfway mark turn over to the
   back and finish the distance
   on any back stroke of your
   choice.
5. Plunge (dive and glide) as far
   as possible.
6. Commencing with the
   appropriate racing start, swim
   25 metres front or back crawl.
7. Commencing with the
   appropriate racing start, swim
   25 metres breast or butterfly
   stroke.

Stage 3

Perform the following in the
order set out:

1. Where possible, dressed in
   trousers and shirt or pyjamas,
   enter the water from the side
   of the pool by a straddle or a
   tuck jump, swim 45 metres.
2. Tread water for 2 minutes in a
   vertical position.
3. Using any floating object for
   support, take up and hold the
   Heat Exposure Lessening
   Posture (H.E.L.P.) for 2
   minutes.
4. Swim 400 metres, surface
   diving once during the swim,
   and swimming at least 5
   metres completely
   submerged. Climb out from
   deep water without assistance
   or the use of steps.

World Conservation

Carry out these projects as a member of a group of Cub Scouts and not by yourself. This group could be your Pack, Six or other small group.

1. While you are working on this badge with your group:
   a) find some examples showing how man has damaged nature and other examples showing how man has improved nature;
   b) find examples of where the Country Code is being broken and the results of this.

2. Take part as a group in two projects, such as :
   a) clearing a ditch, pond or stream;
   b) making, setting up and maintaining a bird feeder, bird table, bird nesting box or bird bath;
   c) cultivating and maintaining a garden and a compost heap;
   d) tidying up a piece of wasteland;
   e) an anti-litter campaign;
   f) plant a tree or shrub.

Note: Other projects may be undertaken as agreed by the Cub Scout Leader.

3. Choose one from the following:
   a) make a display to inform others about an animal, bird, plant, fish, etc. which is in danger of extinction;
   b) organise a 'save it' campaign to encourage others to conserve energy e.g. home insulation, fuel efficient engines, etc;
   c) take part in or start a re-cycling scheme, e.g. bottles, cans, waste paper, etc.
   d) visit a forest, wood or camp site to take part in a project on tree conservation to discover whether any trees have been lost and, if so whether any have been replaced. With expert help, find out how trees can be cared for.

Note: Where Cub Scouts are encouraged to carry out a project anywhere near water, for example, clearing a ditch or pond or carrying out a small fish survey, Leaders must have adequate arrangements for the safety of the Cub Scouts and ensure that the activity is properly supervised.

World Faiths

With the help of a Leader and the agreement of somebody at home do *either* requirement 1 a) or 1 b) and then all of requirement 2.

1. Either:
   a) Make arrangements and visit a place of worship other than your own and find out some information about the building, its contents and its form of worship.

Or:
   b) Meet someone who belongs to a faith or denomination other than your own and discover how they put their faith into practice in their daily life.

2. Find out about a faith other than your own and tell the examiner about any of its sacred books, holy places, religious customs and the dates of special festivals.

World Friendship

Choose any three from the following list:-

1. Be a penfriend to a child from another country and write or send tapes to them for at least three months.

2. Recognise the flags from ten countries in the world, five of which must be from outside the European Community.

3. Collect at least three coins, stamps and postcards from three different countries in the European Community and then discuss with the examiner what you know about the European Community. You will need to find out, for example: where the Parliament Building is, who is your Member of the European Parliament, which countries are in the European Community, what the flag looks like.

4. Write a prayer about world peace and friendship and read it at a Pack meeting or your place of worship.

5. Make a collage, model or chart of the work of the United Nations.

6. Do something to help another country in need at the moment. Perhaps it could be a country that has had severe floods, famine, disease or an earthquake.

7. Draw six National Scout Badges from around the world.

8. Mark a world map to show where all the World Jamborees have been held.

Writer

1. Make and present a collection of stories and/or poems you have written on a variety of themes.
2. Write a report on a recent Cub Scout event for use in a newsletter or magazine and read it to others.
3. Write a letter and address an envelope neatly, and show a knowledge of postcodes and letter postal rates: e.g. a thank you letter, an invitation, a request for help, a letter to a friend, or any other suitable subject.

Activity Badge Record

DATE AWARDED	DATE AWARDED	DATE AWARDED
▷ Animal Lover	▷ Entertainer	▷ Naturalist ....
▷ Artist	▷ Explorer	▷ Navigator ....
▷ Astronomer	▷ First Aider	▷ Personal Safety ....
▷ Athlete	▷ Gardener	▷ Photographer ....
▷ Book Reader	▷ Handyman	▷ Scientist ....
▷ Camper	▷ Health & Fitness	▷ Sportsman ....
▷ Collector	▷ Hobbies	▷ Swimmer ....
▷ Communicator	▷ Home Help	▷ World Conservation ....
▷ Community	▷ Home Safety	▷ World Faiths ....
▷ Computer	▷ Local Historian	▷ World Friendship ....
▷ Cook	▷ Map Reader	▷ Writer ....
▷ Craftsman	▷ Musician	
▷ Cyclist	▷ My Faith	

What's Next? - The Scout Troop!

Well then, what is next? You do want some more fun don't you? Probably you want to move on and try something more grown up and adventurous.

The next group of people in the Family of Scouts is waiting for you in the Scout Troop.

You will have heard about the sort of things that Scouts do. You may have tried one or two of their activities already in your Scout Family Badges and would like to try some more.

Have you heard about camping expeditions, Patrol projects and pioneering? Well, you are about to hear even more once you make contact with the Scout Leader and the Patrol Leaders' Council.

When you visit your Patrol for an activity, you wil probably recognise a lot of things (and faces!). They will still play games and meet regularly, perhaps even in the same place as the Pack, they will still shake hands using their left hand as a sign of greeting and will make the same Scout Sign as the Pack does on special occasions. Of course, you will also recognise the World Membership Badge, the one that all Scouts everywhere wear in one form or another.

Just like you did when you were invested, all Scouts make a Promise and try to keep the Scout Law. In the same way that you wanted a more grown up Promise than the Beaver Scout makes, the Scout Law and Promise is more grown up than the one you are trying to keep at the moment.

The Scout Law

1. A Scout is to be trusted.
2. A Scout is loyal.
3. A Scout is friendly and considerate.
4. A Scout is a brother to all Scouts.
5. A Scout has courage in all difficulties.
6. A Scout makes good use of his time and is careful of possessions and property.
7. A Scout has respect for himself and others.

The Scout Promise

On my honour, I promise that I will do my best to do my duty to God and to the Queen, to help other people and to keep the Scout Law.

Scout Membership Badge

When you are aged around 10½, you should be ready to think about moving into your local Scout Troop. You will also be ready to work for the Scout Membership Badge.

You must be at least ten years old and must complete each section of this badge.

1. Talk with your future Patrol Leader about joining the Troop.
2. Join a Patrol of your liking and get to know the other members by taking part in an activity with them.
3. Get to know the other Scouts and Leaders in the Troop by taking part in at least three Troop Meetings, one of which should be out of doors.
4. Show a general knowledge of the Scout Movement and the development of world wide Scouting.
5. Know, understand and accept the Scout Promise and Law. Talk with a Scout Leader about how you can put them into practice each day.
6. Know what to do at your investiture and, if you would like to, invite someone to be there.

Moving House

If you are going to move house or even go to boarding school you may not be able to carry on being a Cub Scout in the Pack you are in now.

You will probably want to join a Pack in your new area as soon as possible to make new friends quickly and continue with the fun and adventure of Cub Scouting.

To help you find a Pack in your new area, fill in the form printed here and send it to the address given at the bottom. Ask your Leader to give you a copy of your record card so that you can give it to your new Leader.

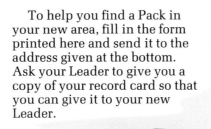

Transfer Form

Name ....

Present Address ....

....

at present a Member of the

....

Cub Scout Pack, will be moving to (full postal address):

....

....

on (date)..................... and wishes to join the nearest suitable Scout Group.

SEND THIS FORM TO:
The Scout Association, Records Office, Churchill Industrial Estate, LANCING, West Sussex BN15 8UG

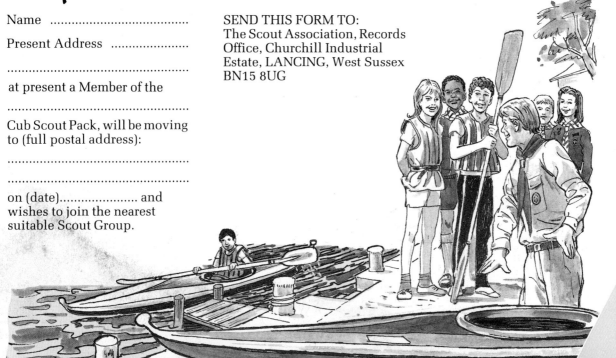

123

Index